As a surgeon who has worked with patients suffering from overeating and with an interest in the neurology and mental processing of emotion, I was very pleased to read this book. It is well researched and academically rigorous yet accessible to the public. It is equally valuable to the student and practitioner. What distinguishes this work from numerous others is the empathetic treatment given to this difficult subject, only possible by an experienced and sensitive therapist. The author is clearly completely in command of her subject and she reflects a deep knowledge of all the psychological swerves that lead to loss of nutritional control. The solutions are sympathetically and persuasively explained and aimed at permanence. I recommend this book as a valuable addition to the literature of disordered eating.

J E G Walker MB; BS: BDS; FDSRCS; MA (Ethics)

In her first book, Kathy Leach wrote for psychotherapists with over-weight patients. Now in her second book, with its accompanying app and supports, Kathy brings her vast breadth of knowledge, experience and compassion directly to the person for whom being overweight is the problem. It contains a combination of clear explanations, inspirational exercises and powerful psychological concepts from transactional analysis. If you are interested in really looking the demon in the eye and embarking on a deep journey of self-exploration and healing, this is the book that could transform not just your body, but your life and the way you think about yourself.

Charlotte Sills MSc *is a psychotherapist, supervisor and trainer in London, UK. She is also Professor of Coaching at Ashridge Business School.*

If you want to understand your relationship with food this book will guide you. Kathy Leach has developed a program that respectfully leads the reader to make the journey back through their experience to discover the reason they eat as they do. Kathy gently leads the reader to understand their process with self-respect and compassion, using a program she has devised based on Transactional Analysis. As a therapist Kathy has much experience of this client group and under-stands the complexities of this subject and in her enlightening book, she confirms that the dilemma is understood and is changeable if you so decide.

Jenny Holmes MBACP, *Therapist and supervisor in private practice.*

T0384882

The Overweight Mind and Body

The Overweight Mind and Body is a self-help guide to understanding the psychological issues that lead to overeating and weight gain.

The book enables the reader to discover the psychological drives that lead to unwanted weight and to find ways of meeting those drives other than with food. It introduces a simple, user-friendly theory of Transactional Analysis to promote weight-related self-awareness. The author includes exercises that empower readers to uncover their own stories. She understands that, for many, carrying extra weight is emotionally and physically painful and so gently encourages readers to explore at their own level. She uses case studies to demonstrate the many unconscious influences on one's eating and how, when people discover and resolve these influences, they no longer need extra food. Reading them shows that "you are not alone".

This book will also be of interest to, and a useful guide for, all practitioners in the caring professions who work with clients struggling with eating and overweight.

Kathy Leach is a training and supervising Transactional Analysis Psychotherapist, who has specialized in working with overweight issues in various capacities since 1980. Initially teaching a holistic approach to weight management and self-care and subsequently training as a psychotherapist researching this area of concern, she has remarkable insight into weight-related challenges.

The Overweight Mind and Body

Your Unique Psychological Journey Towards Weight Loss

Kathy Leach

Routledge
Taylor & Francis Group

LONDON AND NEW YORK

Cover image: © Getty Images

First published 2022

by Routledge
2 Park Square, Milton Park, Abingdon, Oxon OX14 4RN

and by Routledge
605 Third Avenue, New York, NY 10158

Routledge is an imprint of the Taylor & Francis Group, an informa business

© 2022 Kathy Leach

British Library Cataloguing\-in\-Publication Data
A catalogue record for this book is available from the British Library

Library of Congress Cataloguing-in-Publication Data
Names: Leach, Kathy, 1949- author.
Title: The overweight mind and body : your unique psychological journey towards weight loss / Kathy Leach.
Description: Milton Park, Abingdon, Oxon ; New York, NY : Routledge, 2022.
Identifiers: LCCN 2021043470 (print) | LCCN 2021043471 (ebook) | ISBN 9781032147437 (hardback) | ISBN 9781032147420 (paperback) | ISBN 9781003240877 (ebook)
Subjects: LCSH: Obesity--Psychological aspects. | Weight loss--Psychological aspects.
Classification: LCC RC552.O25 L43 2022 (print) | LCC RC552.O25 (ebook) | DDC 616.3/980651--dc23/eng/20211104
LC record available at https://lccn.loc.gov/2021043470
LC ebook record available at https://lccn.loc.gov/2021043471

ISBN: 978-1-032-14743-7 (hbk)
ISBN: 978-1-032-14742-0 (pbk)
ISBN: 978-1-003-24087-7 (ebk)

DOI: 10.4324/9781003240877

Typeset in Times New Roman
by MPS Limited, Dehradun

My thanks to all my very supportive editors, my critics, my endorsers, Charlotte Sills, Jenny Holmes and Graham Walker, my clients from whom I have learnt so much and my very patient, manuscript-checking husband, Tony.

Contents

About the Author: Introducing myself

I am a Training and Supervising Psychotherapist. I work with groups and individuals, and I have for many years worked with people who are, or feel themselves to be, overweight and are discomforted or distressed by their size and eating. I run courses for practitioners in the field and medical services.

My first book: "The Overweight Patient" – A Psychological Approach to understanding and working with Obesity" (published by Jessica Kingsley) has sold very successfully both in English speaking countries and in foreign language translations.

I have worked in the field of weight and eating in various capacities for over 30 years. During this period my understanding of the complexities of this area of focus has grown from my continued involvement with people presenting with a vast range of weight and eating issues.

After my first child, I put on a great deal of weight and the "Which" guide to slimming listed a new organisation called Slimnastics which advocated a holistic approach to weight loss. I joined and lost a lot of weight. I was so impressed with these classes that I first became a teacher and then a teacher trainer and exam moderator for the organisation. The weekly classes involved weight control, healthy eating, stress management, relaxation and lifestyle. The courses were fun and most of the members lost weight although there was no pressure to do so. The combination of exercise at whatever level the participants could manage, healthy eating (no diets) and stress management and relaxation to engender calm and mindfulness, was very powerful. Many people maintained their weight loss far better than in several other slimming groups at the time, where the emphasis was (and still is) on weight loss through prescribed diets or regimes. However, a few did not lose weight and some did put the unwanted weight back on after leaving the classes and I was intrigued to understand why this might have been.

When I trained as a psychotherapist, I made it part of my life's work to research and work psychologically with people who suffer unhappiness due to their weight; to discover as much as I could about the psychological aspects that render people unable to lose weight when they want to or to leave them in need of maintaining an unwanted large body size. In the process, and through psychotherapy, I did, of course, learn a lot about myself. Applying the psychotherapeutic concepts described in this book, I began to understand how I was using food and what my relationship was with my body.

I have been overweight with feelings of self-loathing and a lack of self-worth. I have done the diets and my weight has risen and fallen. I was a fat child and I have been called names and ridiculed. I know what all that feels like. For a while I was bulimic, but of course, though I was thin, it resolved nothing. I have been through this journey. I now maintain my weight within parameters that are right for me, both in my vision of myself and for health reasons. I do go up and down but not by huge amounts and I have a ceiling beyond which I will not allow myself to go.

I do not chastise myself if I gain weight. I know I will take it off if I want to and when I am ready. If we reprimand ourselves, we feel more wretched and are more likely to eat! Empathy and understanding are what we all need from ourselves, and, wherever possible, from others too.

I believe that you can also achieve this level of choice which is why I have been keen to write a book that uses the basic concepts of Transactional Analysis (TA) psychotherapy to help you on your personal journey of understanding, acceptance and change.

Part I

The foundations of your journey towards understanding and change

Chapter 1

Important points to think about as a foundation to your self-exploration

This chapter is an introduction to the main focusses of the book. It sets the groundwork for your journey of self-exploration. Please take your time to read and think about each paragraph and the points in each one. There is no rush! A slow journey allows for deeper understanding and slower weight loss is more likely to be permanent.

This self-help book is written for people who are unhappy about, and struggle with, their eating and weight. It is these people I have worked with psychologically for over 30 years.

My belief is that everyone deserves to be happy and to make their own choices as to how they want to be in the world. You are worth looking after and worth positive attention. You deserve to be who you want to be at whatever size you want to be. You may not feel this is possible right now but if you have this as your aim, you will find the ensuing chapters helpful and rewarding.

In each chapter, you will have the chance to look at what goes on psychologically for you. To see how your past, and others around you now, can influence your thoughts about yourself and about your body and eating. You will see how you have made unhelpful decisions about yourself in response to others both past and present and how to update those decisions.

You can make your own new decisions about how you want to be in the world. Your weight, your size and your eating are nobody else's concern.

There are many aspects contributing to being overweight and overeating when you don't want to be. In this first chapter, I would like to visit some of those with you, starting with practical issues and moving on to the more intricate and intriguing psychological concerns. Some will remain as brief paragraphs in this chapter and others will be the focus of future chapters.

I am trained in, and practise, Transactional Analysis Psychotherapy (TA). It maintains a highly in-depth theory of personality, ways of understanding ourselves and ways of making positive changes in our lives. It enables us to understand what goes on between ourselves and others and within ourselves at both a conscious and unconscious level. A good deal of the language of TA is simple but it can reach the subconscious quite rapidly and sometimes

DOI: 10.4324/9781003240877-1

unexpectedly. It is therefore important for you to think about seeking therapy if challenging or unsettling issues are raised for you that cannot be met in a book.

In this school of psychotherapy, we have some very fundamental beliefs. It is worth thinking about each one and what they can offer for you. They are what I believe about you, others and myself. I have added a daily mantra for each focus of belief. The thinking behind this is that the more you repeat a positive thought, the more likely you are to be open to believing it. Maybe it is not possible for you to fully commit to each one yet, but you can start that upward ladder of belief.

Belief I

That everyone is OK

In other words, everyone is worthy, deserves respect and is essentially good. We may not like what they or, in fact, we do, i.e. the behaviour, but that does not change the stance of everyone having worth and value as human beings. We aim to give everyone a chance. (Historically and internationally, there are some notable exceptions, but they are not you). We believe that we are OK too. "I am OK and you are OK".

Feeling OK is something that is lost for many people struggling with weight. You need to know that you are OK whether you are big, small, fat, thin, tall or short. Just because you have put on unwanted weight does not mean you are not an OK person. Make **"I am OK"** one of your daily mantras. Repeating it will help you believe it and come to know it is true. Part of what we will be exploring is the loss of the feeling of "OKness" because, often, it is that loss that makes us eat and then the extra weight gained can lead to us thinking even more deeply, that we are not OK.

You are OK: This is at the core of you and does not change just because you have put on weight.

So your first daily mantra will be: I am OK.

Belief 2

That everyone can think and decide what is right for themselves

You are an adult. You can make your own mind up about yourself, what you do and how you do it. This may sound obvious and even irrelevant, but as you work through the book, you will see how often your unconscious self will respond to others from the past and present and feel influenced by their thoughts, feelings and behaviours.

Throughout this book I am inviting you to claim back the full you.

When we are reaching for that extra food, we aren't thinking with our grown-up selves. And we are not deciding to eat the food from a rational, grown-up place.

So your second daily mantra is: I can think for myself.

It is interesting that many overweight people feel that, either they cannot think, or that other people don't believe they can think. This, of course, is nonsense. You can think and, as you can think, you can also make decisions for yourself. You can and do make decisions. In fact, from when you were tiny, you have been making decisions about yourself, other people and the world around you, even though you have not been conscious of doing so. Some of these decisions have been made when you were too young to be rational and many of these types of decisions remain in operation until you re-decide or change those decisions. For example, many overweight people have decided at some stage in the past that they are not worth bothering about. It is irrational because everyone is essentially worthy. Or perhaps they have decided that they need to look after others' needs and wants and so must never put themselves first. Though this might be seen as admirable, we are entitled to think about our own needs. The need to please others can lead to self-neglect and self-denial. With new information and a little thought, these decisions can be changed. They are not set in concrete as people often believe. With some personal understanding, you can decide anew and that is what you will be encouraged to do throughout this book. So the third belief is that your past decisions are free to be amended.

Belief 3

Decisions made in the past can be changed and new, valid, decisions made

In TA, we consider what decisions we have made about ourselves, others and the world, even from infancy. We make decisions in response to who is, and what is going on, around us. The beauty of this is that we can re-decide once we have understood what is behind the decisions that are no longer helpful or appropriate. You will find that a good deal of the time you are acting in response to what has gone on in the past and particularly in childhood, even from infancy. You will discover that you often respond to a parent in the same way you did as a child. You may find you still carry out their "orders", such as "clean your plate", "if you don't do as I say you won't have a treat". Often we continue to do what we were told to do as kids, some of it very helpful and some of it restricting. And we may repeat the same "orders" to our own children! You may recall some of the orders in your household and will be encouraged to look at these in later chapters.

We also behave in accordance with what we think others expect of us and this is not always helpful. For instance, if you are out with friends do you eat less and then eat more when you get home? Do you get anxious about eating in public because you think others will be watching and judging you? Do you eat secretly? hide food? Pick when no-one is looking?

In the past, we may have *decided*, because of family sayings, or social opinions, that, if we are "overweight", we are not good enough. We are not deserving. This again is so unhelpful and certainly not true.

In addition, it is common for people struggling with weight to think they shouldn't do things, such as swim, dance, wear bright clothes, or shorts. Is this familiar to you?

(I discuss the use of the term overweight in chapter 3.)

If you can think for yourself, then you clearly have choices. You can decide what you choose to do. Your thinking in this book will be geared to **understanding** why you eat extra food or are overweight. Once you get this understanding you can make new decisions about yourself, food and weight. There are always choices, even if it doesn't feel like it at this moment.

So your third daily mantra is: I can make my own decisions for myself and about myself.

A battle with food?

I often find that people who consider themselves overweight have a sense of food being both a comfort and an enemy, hence the words "struggle" and "battle". We will look at the food being a comfort later in the book but here I want to make the statement for you that food is not your enemy. It is what you need in order to survive, to live your daily life and to thrive. For this reason food is your friend.

What is important to consider is this: **If you do not have an enemy, you cannot have a battle.**

If **food is not your enemy** then you do not need to create a battle with it. The struggle that goes on in your head over food is counterproductive. You will learn that you have different sides of yourself that play their part in "making" you eat; One part is called Child, and another is your Parent. It is usually your Child self that wants, or even feels that she/he needs, food beyond your biological needs; That is to say, it is the Child self that holds erroneous beliefs about self, others and the world around it and feels the pain that leads to using food to resolve emotional issues. Sometimes it is the Parent self that tries to deny the Child this food. Once this dialogue of contradictions between Parent and Child selves is set up in your mind, the Child pushes for the extra food and this gives rise to compulsive and impulsive eating.

In the beginning, I suggest you can allow yourself to eat what you wish so that this Inner Child calms, because when thinking of stopping that Inner Child from eating, she/he becomes more agitated and leads you to eat more. Since the pathways I suggest for your journey do not include diets your

Child self will not encounter deprivation. You will, hopefully, feel calmer. There won't be the urgency that is produced by the Child always being told "no" or being made to feel guilty, weak-willed, or even disgusting when eating. Until we have discussed a number of aspects of your eating and possible psychological reasons for your need to overeat, it is best that you feel OK about what you do eat. This is not, however, an invitation to eat more and more but to feel Ok about what you eat now, knowing you are going to learn what that food means to you.

Many people I have worked with have experienced real relief on hearing the suggestion that they can eat what they want as a first stage. Many have found that through this permission they already started to eat less because there is no sense that they might not be able to have that food at all. In addition the messages that tell someone they shouldn't eat the food often result in more agitation or rebellion against that command which leads toactually eating more. Overeating is regularly seen to follow conscious or unconscious anxiety that there will not be enough, a sense of deprivation or scarcity. In most parts of the world, there is always enough food and it is never far away. I suggest that you are rarely very far from food outlets and shops, even if your fridge and cupboards are empty. So there is no likelihood of there "not being enough".

I have only once found that a client couldn't bear the thought of being able to eat what she wanted at this stage of the journey. It made her feel angry and scared. If this is also your response, then you need to stay with the way you think about food at present. That will be fine too.

If you have been eating a lot of extra food, you have essentially been eating what you want but, no doubt, accompanied by all the negative feelings. When we get a feeling or "message" in our heads that says "you can't eat that" we are more likely to rebel and eat more of it. Then, self-deprecating messages often follow. Sometimes these are accompanied by feelings of guilt at best and maybe self-loathing at worst. So why not have permission to eat what you want instead? You may continue to eat in the same pattern, or you might find some of the pressure is off and you auto-matically reach for that extra food less often. Either way it would be good to write down your experiences about this "permission". You can do so at the end of this chapter.

You will see that I do not recommend "dieting" and that there is no call to change your eating habits until you have explored why you are "overeating" or maintaining a larger body size. After all, the purpose of this self-guided book is to enable you to understand your eating. If you resolve underlying issues, your eating will change.

You will be encouraged to use healthy eating that is right for you rather than follow a fixed regime dictated by someone else. If you feel you **ought** to go to a slimming group, (which would be a Parent message) then it is likely you will not keep off the weight you may lose. "Oughts" and "Shoulds" that plague you from within, from other people in your life and from our cultural messages are exceedingly unsupportive. If you go to a slimming group because you have been persuaded to go or you feel you should in order to be OK with other people, then you are more likely to sabotage yourself and put any weight loss back on. And, people often put on more pounds than before after each arrested diet phase. If there are psychological reasons as to why you carry more weight than you want and eat more food than you want and need, then those reasons must be attended to before your goal weight loss can be achieved and maintained.

If you have struggled with your unwanted weight for some lengthy time, there are clearly reasons why you have done so.

As I have said, what feels like hunger for food is often actually hunger for something else. The sensations can feel the same, but if you have eaten a full meal, it is unlikely you are in need of food within the next few hours. If you feel hungry when you have had a good meal then it is almost certainly what we call a psychological hunger, not a biological one, which is just about having enough "fuel" to go about your day. We will be exploring this together so that you can begin to determine whether you want and need food or whether it is something else. If it is something else, the "comfort" effect of eating will only ever be short-lived.

Choice

As the grown-up you are, you will always have a choice. Sometimes it doesn't feel like there is a choice or that you have been making choices. However, if we accept that we have been choosing our way in life, it is much easier to think about making other new choices. We do have to keep in mind that some of our choices have been unconscious or driven by what has happened and what we have experienced in the past. Overeating may be one such choice. Needing to be bigger in the world is another psychologically driven choice. This is why it is so important to understand what is driving you to remain overweight when you don't want to be. If you have dieted in the past, you have made a choice. If you have stopped the diet it was another choice. But these choices are wrapped up in unconscious messages and processes. You do have a choice to eat more or less and you have a choice to lose weight or not. Throughout your journey it is important to know that you HAVE been choosing and making decisions, much of the time from your unconscious. Every action has involved a choice by you and those choices have been made for good reasons despite bringing discomfort. It may be hard to accept this idea but, you have at some level chosen to be overweight for good reasons and you have chosen to eat extra food, again for good reasons. By bringing your choices, and the reasons behind them, into your awareness, you have an opportunity to consider them and you can make new choices and new decisions about what you do from an adult and discerning place. The chapters in this book take you through a journey of enquiry into what has made you unconsciously choose to eat and be over-weight even though it causes you discomfort and distress.

Never compare yourself with anyone else. You are uniquely you. Know what is right for you and know this because you are OK and you are worth it. What you want is paramount and no one else can tell you how you should be. That is not to say you can't have a buddy to work with on your journey, but do remember it is not a competition and there is no failure. There is simply your ongoing journey towards your own chosen goal.

Blips are allowed

Blips are allowed! They do not mean all is lost! Never think that if you have a day or two when you have not made your adult choices about eating that you have failed. We all have off days. We all have times when the gremlins take over and knock us off track. We just have to get back on our track and continue the journey. Always think of going forward and resuming your journey.

In later chapters, you will see how you can turn a blip into a positive as it presents an opportunity to look at why that blip has arisen. Something will have happened to cause you to have a few challenging days when you might revert to old patterns of eating. You will learn how to look at what has gone on before eating that extra food or turning away from your journey.

A question you will be able to ask yourself is "Am I hungry for food or do I need something else?"

I hope that as a result of working through this book you will eventually be able to readily think about food choices and make your own decisions about eating or not. You will not eat impulsively or compulsively, because those behaviours are the old way. You will make your food and weight decisions from a place of feeling OK, good enough and worth it.

Our aim, then, is to enable you to understand yourself in relation to food and body size; to move towards respecting and caring for yourself. We will discuss psychological hungers and you will become aware of the difference in sensations between when you are biologically hungry and when you are psychologically hungry, for instance, hungry for something missing or un-satisfying in your life. Psychological hungers are to do with emotionally based needs and their related behavioural and physical needs.

As you work through your journey, you may experience a variety of emotions including fear, anger, sadness and joy and a whole spectrum of internal dialogues. Don't be afraid of feelings. You can view them as useful information. You never need to do anything you do not want to do or are not ready to do. If you do find your feelings and thoughts are becoming overwhelming, please seek help from a trained therapist or counsellor.

You will be invited to reflect on and write down your thoughts and feelings regularly throughout the course of the book. You might want to buy yourself an attractive notebook in which to write down thoughts and feelings as you work through the tasks presented. There are a few pages at the back of the book for this purpose and there are spaces for you to write answers to questions on some pages, but it might be that, as you increase your momentum, you might want to reflect and write more than the spaces allow.

After each chapter and task, I know it will be immensely helpful for you to spend a little time looking at what you have written and think about it. Be curious! This is an exciting journey. Never be judgemental. Everything you do, think and feel is important.

So, here is a good place to start! Write down a few words and sentences if you wish, in response to what you have read so far. Reflect on them in an inquisitive and interested way. Be kind to, and supportive of, yourself. Aim to write positive thoughts. If you want to write something that is not positive, then be sure to write more positives than negatives. Positivity works wonders.

My thoughts on permission to eat:

My positive thoughts so far:

I like:

I want to:

I certainly will:

A further word of caution

As you work through the chapters you will be asked to look at issues that are causing you to eat more than you really want to and to carry more weight than you want to. Recognising these issues by bringing them to consciousness can be challenging or even, at times, feel distressing. You will be guided in how to keep yourself safe and OK and you also clearly have the option to work through some of the tasks and chapters with a counsellor or therapist.

You need to keep yourself safe

If you should become distressed:

1. Stop the exercise you are doing, or stop reading.
2. Take a few really deep breaths and relax your muscles.
3. Talk to someone else, either face to face or make a phone call. You could talk about what you are experiencing or something completely different.
4. It often helps to go and wash your hands and face in warm or cold water.
5. Find something involving to do for a while. This could be chores, errands, puzzles, writing down your thoughts, drawing a picture of some kind, listening to music, or perhaps escaping with something absorbing on TV or the internet. I am sure you can add to this list.
6. Think about the fact that you have survived. You have survived whatever has been triggered from the past and you have survived this moment. Reassure yourself of this. You know how to survive and so you can use that knowledge to survive now.
7. When you feel more settled, be interested in what you have been feeling.
8. Before you return to your journey, (maybe a few days later) make sure you are in the here and now and recognise you are an adult and can think. You can think through what you have experienced. It may be that you want to have someone with you.
9. Do not continue with the exploratory chapters if you are fearful of what you have discovered or what you will discover. Seek professional help. You must be responsible for your own decisions in this regard.
10. This book is about finding out what is driving you, against your will, to overeat. It can help you to focus on issues with a psychotherapist if that is what you choose to do.

Chapter 2

You are worth it

One of the barriers to making changes about food and eating with many of my clients has been their belief that they are not worth it. They believe they do not deserve to be happy or to spend time on themselves and they often have low self-esteem.

I hold the belief that you are worth it in the same way that I believe that everyone is fundamentally OK; I am OK and you are OK. And that everyone can think and can make choices and decisions.

Try saying, and repeating

"I am worth it"

In TA we use a contractual method. This means we make a contract with our clients as to what we are doing in the psychotherapy space and what the goals are. This is very helpful as it does keep us on track and it is made between us as equals in the process. I would like to make a contract with you that you tell yourself each day that you are worth it. Add this to the other three mantras that we discussed in chapter 1. "I am OK"; "I can think for myself"; "I can make my own decisions for myself and about myself"; "I have choices".

This means you are worth the care and attention you are going to give yourself as you work through this journey.

- It means you deserve to be happy and to achieve what makes you happy; this includes being the right size for you.
- It means you understand your own worth and that no one else can take that away from you.
- It means you are worth spending your time reading these chapters and doing the corresponding tasks and answering the questions, applying them in your daily life and valuing both yourself and what you are doing as your journey continues.
- As you grow in your belief that you are worth it, so others will respond to you accordingly.

DOI: 10.4324/9781003240877-2

When you get up in the morning, start with your mantras. Start and end with **"I am worth it"**. You can write down at the back of the book anything that comes into your head as you say this. Be intrigued.

It is not always easy to say "I am worth it" but the more you repeat it, the more it will sink in that you really are **"worth it"**.

A second contract I would like to offer is that you agree **that you do not give up.** That you don't give up on your journey if you have a little lapse or forget something. Blips will occur, but they are only blips, no matter how big they appear at the time. There is no such thing as a failure on this journey. Any difficult days are just part of the onward journey and provide useful information in your understanding of yourself. Later chapters guide you in how to use these challenging days as important elements in your self-discovery.

Imagine yourself walking on a smooth easy road, going somewhere nice where you will be happy. This is the road to the new you. Then suddenly there are boulders and rocks on the road. Do you stop your journey, even though the place ahead would bring you happiness? Do you give up and go back to the dark place you came from? Or do you climb over the boulders and rocks and, having got over those hurdles, head to that sunny place again?

If you have dieted and stopped many times in the past maybe you have just had to go back and set out again at a later date, never quite getting there. This time, you are going to find the rocks and boulders and climb over them and you are going to continue on the road to your success. Keep going forward. You will soon access your clear road again. It is there for you. Don't be discouraged.

Because "**You are worth it.**"

Chapter 3

Overeating and overweight –
What do they mean?

I hope the term "overeating" is a helpful one if we think of it as basically eating more than is needed for daily living and a little more for unexpected emergencies. However, in our culture, we eat a good deal more than that because we can, but the message remains the same. We do not need so much food that we carry extra fat around our bodies. To those who don't want that extra weight, it becomes a menace, drags us down physically and mentally and can make life miserable as well as possibly being harmful to health.

Unless you are at risk of health complications by remaining the size you are, then you are overweight when you are heavier than you want to be. To me, it is as simple as that. (This, of course, excludes those who are anorexic and want to be thinner than is healthy for them.) If your weight prevents you from living the life you want to live, keeps you in a place of lack of self-worth, induces lack of confidence, limits your desired level of activity and socialising, then, yes, you will benefit from weight loss. Or you might, with reflection and investigation, come to feel happy the size you are now. You have that choice.

Recognising your overeating

It is a really good idea for you to think about **when** you eat those extra foods, whether you pick at things or have a large plate of food, or seconds and thirds, or snacks between meals.

I invite you to think about this now, as it will help you to start to think about whether you are eating to satisfy biological hunger or in response to emotional or stressful times. This separation between biological hunger and psychological hunger allows us to look at what issues we need to resolve or accept. I address this idea fully in chapter 9.

Think now about your day from rising in the morning to bedtime and see if you can list when it is you eat extra foods. Some suggestions might be: eating everything on your plate, a very common parental message, or do you have those little tasters whilst cooking or preparing food? Do you snack in

DOI: 10.4324/9781003240877-3

front of the TV or between meals? Are there foods from childhood you crave and eat? Once you become aware of your eating patterns you might be quite surprised at how these extras add up. But more importantly, that awareness will allow you to see how you use food which gives you the groundwork for exploration in later chapters.

How and when I eat extra food. Jot down your list here or in your own book. Be as honest as you can. You don't need to share this with anyone unless it helps to do so.

You have now brought these realities very much into your AWARENESS.

Awareness is a key factor in becoming the size you want to be and are comfortable with. You will become more and more aware as you continue your journey. A good deal of what we do is automatic and habitual and basically outside of awareness. It is when we are aware and conscious of what we are doing that we can make changes.

Your goal must be achievable. Do not head for a skinny prince or princess – that is for fairy tales and the fashion industry. Aim for a size you are comfortable with and can maintain. One that suits you well.

What I would like to propose is that you:

- Trust yourself. You can know what is right for you.
- Decide for yourself what you want and decide on a weight and size that is right for you and is not about what other people think or say.
- **Choose** a weight and size that is comfortable for you that does not risk your health, your mobility, and your desires for your life.

This is a realistic, respectful and caring approach. There is no pressure (unless you are at risk with your health) and no competition; just you doing what you want to do, how and when you want to do it. No one else matters in this. This is for you.

Chapter 4

The psychological reasons for unhurried weight loss

Research shows that losing weight slowly is always better than losing large amounts very quickly. Firstly your body has time to get used to a gradual change and secondly your psychological self needs time, not only to accommodate to a smaller size but to resolve issues that have caused eating extra food or holding on to a bigger size. Clients who have been on fast-track abstention diets and have subsequently come to my therapy groups have reported feeling very fragile and anxious, in some extreme cases, even believing that they would be blown away in the wind or will disappear completely. So, from the exhilaration of their fast weight loss, they became fearful and all these clients had started to regain weight, some binge eating, in order to feel safe within that illusionary protection offered by being bigger. This is when they looked for psychotherapy treatment. Gradual change is ideal, not just because the body can adjust to the changes, but because the mind, or psychological self, can also customise to the changes at a gradual and manageable rate.

If weight loss is too fast it is very likely that the weight will be regained. If it is slow it is much more possible to be permanent. 1–2 pounds/0.5–1 kg per week is a very good weight loss. Yo-yo dieting automatically makes it harder to lose weight long term. Often clients who have yo-yo dieted for many years have found that they have invariably put on extra weight each time, such that they are always heavier than the last time they started a diet. My explanation for this is that the weight was there for psychological reasons which had not been resolved. Therefore, not only could they not maintain their weight loss but their unconscious psychological selves that need the weight would add to the imagined protection by gaining more pounds, thus making it more difficult next time! This may sound bizarre, but it is a particularly useful way of thinking about what is going on.

When people lose weight quickly on abstention (such as food packs) diets they may be disposed to dependence on artificial foods and feel fearful when trying to eat normally again. My client, Sophia, had become so dependent on food packs that she was scared to give them up; She no longer knew how to eat normally. She believed that she didn't know what

DOI: 10.4324/9781003240877-4

to eat or how much to eat and became very scared and tearful when discussing giving up food substitutes.

The Inner Child self is the part of us that most needs the extra food and weight. Like any real child, she or he needs us to hear his or her story and to respond with love and caring and with a plan to resolve the issues in an empathic and reliable way. Without such a plan this Inner Child self will eventually experience severe anxiety, especially if the seemingly much-needed food is suddenly withdrawn. There is no time for him or her to feel safe in letting go of the food or weight. Slow weight loss allows that Child-self time to feel safe at each small stage. Underlying psychological issues still need attention alongside this slow weight loss in order to allay the risk of regaining weight. If they are not resolved enough, there will be a point at which the Child-self will become fearful and will rebel against the new, normal food regime. Slow weight loss can be achieved alongside the journey into awareness of underlying issues; fast weight loss does not give enough time for this psychological change to take place.

Many of my clients have automatically begun to eat less once they started to resolve issues in their lives. They have not had to think about a diet or even, at times, plan to eat less. When they felt the reduction in stress and agitation, there was a corresponding reduction in the need for food to quell those feelings. Reduction in the need for food will automatically lead to weight loss.

A key decision is to treat yourself with patience, care and understanding and lose weight slowly.

Chapter 5

How might you sabotage your journey to weight loss?

It may seem a strange thing to ask when you have bought this book and are reading through with the intention of, perhaps, losing weight through self-exploration and understanding but it is an important question. How might you sabotage your journey and your goals?

We know that your unwanted weight and patterns of overeating are in response to unconscious psychological and conscious beliefs about yourself, others and the situation you are in. It is therefore likely that a part of that unconscious self is going to try to sabotage your weight loss and any positive change in eating behaviour. It will try to keep things as they are. We could say it is not going to give in that easily! There are some things you can readily be aware of as to why you eat extra food. It only takes a bit of additional attention to what has just happened before you reach for that food to learn what stimulus was in action. However, how we deal with that knowledge is not always straight forward as you will discover from reading the chapters and completing the tasks in this book. We often discount our ability to do anything because of some psychological message about ourselves, others or our environment. The greater the unconscious fear of change, the greater the need to sabotage will be! You need to believe, and then know, that nothing dreadful is going to happen if you lose your unwanted weight. You will survive without your extra armour as you have survived to this moment.

One way to sabotage yourself is to believe that if you slip up on what you have decided to do, all is lost. There may be good reasons why you have done this and so here is a time when you need to refer to your notes and tasks and to aim to understand what has got in the way. Certainly, all is not lost! You must be sympathetic with yourself. Don't think about starting again; think about continuing your journey when you are ready. Maybe you are climbing around those rocks for a while. If you look back along the track you can see how far you have come and once you have sorted out how to navigate the rocks you can continue onwards. Do not lose heart. Congratulate yourself on what you *have* done and be understanding about what you may not have done. Build on your positives.

DOI: 10.4324/9781003240877-5

It is important for you to understand what shape your sabotage might take and what you need to look out for.

The best way to do this is for you to think about how you are most likely to **not** stick to your plan, then look at your answers and make a list of what you will look out for and what you will do about it next time in order to stick **with** your plan, even if that involves taking a short break. Then be sure to stay thinking about this positive stance.

Use the questions below to guide you.

The past

Think for a moment or two about how you might have given up your weight goals in the past.

What has made you stop your journey in the past? Write as many things as possible.

Now cross out all those things you employed in order to stop yourself in the past. You no longer need them.

The future

What do you need to be aware of to ensure you stay on your journey this time?

How will you ensure you continue your journey to your goal? (Start your answer with "I will ...)

Who, or what might you connect with to help you if you hit one of your sabotages? (Start your answer with I will ...)

Write down the mantras from chapters 1 and 2 **that will help you most.**

By crossing out the thoughts, feelings and events that have stopped you in the past, you allow space for your positive choices. You may still have those negative thoughts from time to time but now you are much more aware of them and you have positive options to think about and guide you.

Now you have discovered the sorts of things that get in the way of staying with your plan, you can be much more aware of when those things are about to happen again. You must be kind to yourself and you must not think that one or two blips ruin the whole journey. Take your time; don't overeat as a reaction to having a couple of off-days. You don't fail, you don't go back. You just resume from where you left off and go forward.

As you work through the chapters, you will gain a lot more understanding of your conscious and unconscious actions. This checklist will help in your choice not to give up on yourself.

> Be understanding and empathic.
> Be patient with yourself.
> Feel your own power.
> Trust yourself.
> Love yourself.
> Don't lose heart.
> Tomorrow is a new day.
> Whatever happens is a valid and informative part of your journey.

Chapter 6

You are not alone

When working with groups both in psychotherapy and on training courses two kinds of "feelings of relief" have often arisen. One is that "there are others who are suffering in the same way as me" and the other is "it is so good to know that someone really understands". Feeling alone with problematic weight issues is a painful experience. Our UK and similar societies have championed slimness for decades and ideal body shapes for centuries. This makes it very difficult for people who are unhappy with their size to talk about their pain. As you work through this book remember that many others are reading it and completing the tasks alongside you.

Here are some stories of people I have worked with. They will affirm that you are not alone and will support other chapters relating to Psychological Hungers, indicating some of the reasons people reach for food in an illusionary attempt to resolve problems. You will notice that I have included cases where the client needed to hold on to a large body size, and, of course, needed food to maintain this. The studies are necessarily brief and only included to illustrate some of the psychological reasons that lead people to be overweight and "overeat" and feel unable to do anything about it. The names are fictitious and the details are those of a number of clients who have presented with the same issues. This ensures that no one is identifiable.

Mark's story. Mark was a twin but, sadly, his brother died after about 10 days. Mark always felt as though there was "something" missing in his life but never understood what this could be. He was never told about his twin and only found out when a cousin, who had been living abroad, came back to the UK. The cousin mentioned Mark's twin, not knowing that he had never been told about him. This was a tremendous shock to Mark. In therapy, we were able to work through his consequent anger, sadness and grief. Mark had been eating in order to fill that empty half of himself. He had felt a deep void but had never realised what it meant. Mark allowed himself to grieve for, and feel his separateness to, his absent twin. Although he continued to feel that he was missing his "other half", Mark was able to accept this in a more age-appropriate way and to decide that he no longer needed to fill that part of him with food.

DOI: 10.4324/9781003240877-6

June's story. In June's family, her mother had "ruled" with food. She praised "good behaviour" with a smile and chocolates or sweets. She showed her displeasure by withholding food. At times she would not let June have lunch or dinner whilst younger siblings were given meals. She also often gave treats to the others which June saw as highlighting her mother's withdrawal of food for her. She would often give them chocolate before bed and June recalled many times when she was offered an apple instead. In her grown-up years, June had unconsciously decided to use food to reward herself but also to deal with stressful situations, rather than deny herself as her mother had done. Gradually June began to recognise the part food was playing for her. She discovered she used food in two ways: One to reward herself when she felt she deserved it, as her mother had done with her siblings, and the other, to give herself food to compensate for when things were not going well, or she felt distressed, as a way of counteracting her mother's withdrawal of food. Her understanding of this pattern of behaviour enabled June to make changes. She no longer used food as a reward or as compensation.

Rowena's story. Rowena was the youngest of four children. Rowena's mother had been ill soon after giving birth and died when she was a baby. Her father never talked about her mother; hence Rowena felt she couldn't ask about her either. She formulated the idea that her mother had died because she didn't love Rowena. Rowena also decided that if her mother didn't love her, she must be unlovable. Further, it made sense to Rowena that her father didn't talk about her mother because she (Rowena) was unlovable. Through therapy, Rowena was able to re-decide and state very clearly that she was (is) lovable. It became clear that Rowena's need for love and to feel lovable had been transferred to food. Feeding is the earliest demonstration of love and care, alongside attunement to the baby's needs, holding and mirroring. Because of her illness and subsequent death, Rowena's mother had not been able to do this long enough for Rowena to internalise her mother's love and her own lovability. She had replaced this with food. Working with her Inner Child self, Rowena was eventually able to claim her lovability. She then decided she needed to talk to her father about her mother and why he had never spoken of her. He said that he hadn't talked about their mother for fear of upsetting Rowena and her siblings. This led to open discussions and sharing of memories and Rowena's relief was profound. In this way, she had further confirmation of her lovability from her father. She soon realised she was already eating less because of these discoveries.

Steven's story. Steven had an "older" father who was very busy working at his own business. His mother had a part-time job but also helped in his father's business. There was little time for Steven once he was past the toddler stage. His father always praised Steven when he finished all the food on his plate, both main course and dessert. If they ate out, he would champion his son when he could eat an adult's portion and would accompany his praise with amiable laughter and smiles. Steven learnt that food was a way of getting attention from his dad. The more he ate the more it seemed to Steven that he was loved and wanted. Steven had little self-esteem. He was the biggest child in his class at school and became ashamed of his body. His dilemma was that he needed to please his dad and therefore he needed to eat. In his therapeutic journey, he realised that he could, as a grown-up, make a new decision for himself about his eating. He came to recognise that he was fulfilling a dynamic in the relationship with his father that not only no longer existed but was never the truth. He was not loved just because he could eat large portions. His father was no longer laughing at and praising his capacity for large amounts of food. He had been following this pattern unconsciously for many years as an adult. On this realisation, he chose to reduce his food intake and lose weight. He did this gradually as he "tested out" his father's love for him until he was sure in himself that that love was there regardless.

Mary's story. Mary was a middle-aged woman who had been "seriously overweight" (her words) for many years. In fact, she had been gaining weight since she was a child. After many sessions, when she felt she could trust me, she told me about an incident of sexual abuse. The abuse was that she had been walking home from school one day and a man had asked her to help him look for his kitten which he thought had gone into the alleyway behind his house. He had presented as upset and so she followed him. When in the alleyway he had lifted her skirt and touched her between the legs, asking her if she liked that. She was very scared and didn't know how to get away. When footsteps were heard on the street, the man let her go and she ran home. She went into the garden and sat in an "old greenhouse", feeling ashamed and scared that someone might find out. The first time she had told this to anyone was in one-to-one therapy with me forty-two years after the abuse had occurred. No one saw her distress which compounded her feelings of shame. Mary recognised that her weight was her defence against abusive men. Having never talked about the abuse before, she had not had any opportunity to resolve her shame and place blame where it was due. Instead, she had decided to keep armour around her body in order to both keep "evil abusers" away and to hide what she imagined to be her "bad self" inside.

Reflections

Take a moment to write down a few brief thoughts and feelings in relation to the stories you have just read.

What do you notice about what you have written?

I will now include remarks my clients have made. I have written each one under a heading that I feel most describes the content. Each one of these clients has been able to work through their psychological issues and to make new decisions, new choices and, those who have wanted to have lost weight.

Read through them and notice what reactions you have. You can write down your thoughts and feelings at the end of the quotations.

Shame

I feel so ashamed. I am ashamed of my body and my eating. I tend to eat privately when no one is around. But you can't hide what you have done. It is there: fat sitting on my body as if it is proud. It has won. I do feel my body. I am so aware of my fat. I feel as though I have many double chins; I have handles around my waist. My boobs are too big because they are fat, fat, fat. I can feel it across my back above my waist and on my bum and inside of my legs. I am gross.

Reward

Often when I have been really busy at work and have not had time to eat a meal, I will go to a service station and pick up bars of chocolate to soothe myself. I think I deserve it when I have worked so hard. But I will still have a meal when I get home. It is so stupid; I am so stupid.

Fear of deprivation

Whenever I go out in my car, whether the journey is short or long, I take food with me. ... just in case... I could not go anywhere without my snacks or sandwiches in my car. I don't always find I need them but I eat them anyway as I don't like waste.

An internalised message

I have to eat everything on my plate, no matter where I am or who I am with. I hate waste. Sometimes I know I have had enough but will continue to eat until my plate is clean. Then I will still eat pudding. When I was a kid, I couldn't have pudding if I didn't eat my main course. It was like a reward. My mother always told us to finish our dinner; she'd say that if we couldn't finish dinner then we must be too full to have a pudding. I do sometimes feel that my trousers are tight but I will carry on.

Self-worth

My father didn't like me being overweight as a child even though he was fat himself. My sister was thin and everyone took notice of her when she walked into a room. No one took any notice of me. I was invisible even though I was a fat child. It is amazing to think that you can feel invisible whilst being big. I don't feel anyone has respect for me when I am bigger. I know that is me; my friends don't actually treat me any different now, whether I am fat or thin. But I feel less confident with them and everyone else if I am my big self. All those names like lazy, out of control, thick, stupid, sloppy, smelly, all apply to me when I am bigger. I hate that. I am worthless unless I am slim.

Prejudice

Everywhere you look there are people who despise overweight people. Even the government is against us. They put out information as to how much we are costing the country. People can call you names, discriminate against you, not offer you a job or promotion, because of being fat. Even discrimination against age is illegal now but not against fat discrimination. We can be bullied, talked about and even spat at and no one cares. It all makes me feel even more wretched and makes me eat more.

Feeling lonely

When I feel lonely, I eat. Often when I sit down in the evening I get the urge to just eat. Anything! It is as though my body is shaky and I have to eat. Sometimes I feel alone even though there are others around. Either way, I just want to eat.

The voices in my head

I don't allow myself to hear the voices in my mind that would tell me to stop eating. At these times, the voices are a long way off. In any case, I can get to the point where I tell them to F... off! I find myself saying "Leave me alone". Sometimes I can believe that those voices just don't know how I feel and so they can keep their advice to themselves. It is horrible. It is like getting one over on the voices. I don't hear them as helpful, just absolutely unable to understand what I feel.

Desperation

When I binge eat, I can eat a bag full of food. I lose myself in eating. The world around me is a blur. I have no idea what is around me; no idea of what is in the room. I am just intent on going through the bag of food; usually, I am on the floor. I can't hear or see anything else. I don't even taste the food. When I am done, I curl up and wait. I am in pain. I am nobody and nothing, except the pain. I know I am here, I am alive, just alive, because of the extreme hurt. Slowly I feel anguish and just want to disappear; to not exist at all. I wonder why I have done it but that never helps me to not do it next time because I get onto the slide that takes me to the pits of despair and it all happens again.

I eat to shut myself up

I now notice that when I feel really on edge, maybe someone has just said something to me that sounds aggressive, or critical, I reach for food. It often doesn't matter what, as long as I put something in my mouth. Sometimes it needs to be chocolate or sweet things. Often it has to be chewable, never sloppy stuff. I know I am stopping myself from speaking; like I might want to be angry; I eat my words so that I don't say them. In the moment of eating, the food clams me up. And then I feel like shit because it is as though I can feel the weight going on in an instant. Talking about it now makes me feel sad.

Tomorrow

I go to bed at night thinking I will do better tomorrow. I will not eat and I feel positive. I wake up in the morning and I feel depressed. My mind immediately goes to food and I begin the constant picking. Sometimes I just need it urgently.

Emptiness

When I am stressed or upset, it feels like my body divides. I feel lost and detached. I have my head and my heart available but my gut, or core, is empty. I guess I just eat to try to fill it up.

Dissociation

Sometimes, when I am eating, I lose everything around me. All I have is my mouth and my body and my body has no feeling. I don't think I even taste the food. I don't have any idea what I am feeling because I feel nothing.

Vulnerability

I can feel the fat around my body, and I feel sturdy. I hate it, loathe it and myself too, but somehow it lets me know I exist and feel I can, at least physically, face the horrid things. I often feel more powerful being big, it comes in handy. But underneath I feel so small and vulnerable.

Eating to the point of discomfort

I frequently eat until I feel sick or so blown up I become uncomfortable; it's even painful at times. I have no idea when to stop before then. That dreadful feeling is when I know to stop eating. I want to stop that and to know when I have had enough but the idea of that also scares me.

Bulimia

I binge eat and then I am ill. I know you have told me to own what I do and that I am not ill when I make myself sick but actually choose to make myself sick. It is hard to admit it is me who is doing it. I try to keep it secret. I do know that it is very bad for me in many ways but it feels good to vomit. At one level it feels good to keep my weight in check like this; on another it does feel self-harming. I feel the confusion.

Now, if it is right for you, look at the following questions and write down your responses.

Questions

1.   Take a moment to describe your thoughts and feelings.

2.   Which of the quotations impacted you most?

3.   Look at your responses in question 2 and see if you can write down why they impacted you.

4. Reflect for a moment on what you have learnt from this and why you will find this useful on your journey.

Finally, whilst we are looking at what people say, let us look at some unhelpful and incorrect beliefs. I have added my responses to each one.

> I can't stop myself eating. *(You can and you are able to learn how)*
> I can't be rude and not eat food that is given to me or made for me. *(Refusal is not rude)*
> I have to say yes when my mum cooks for me, and she cooks a lot. *(No you don't, you are an equal adult and can make your own decisions)*
> I get faint if I don't eat something at least every one to two hours. *(This is not normally true unless there is a medical reason for this, so best check with a doctor)*
> I am always hungry. *(You are unlikely to always be hungry for food)*
> Fat runs in the family. *(Maybe others are big but you still have a choice)*
> I have always been overweight. *(Is it always? Can you think when it actually started?)*
> I can't wear shorts or a bathing costume. *(Who says? Go for it!)*
> I can't dance because of my weight; people would just laugh at me. *(Of course you can dance, don't let anything stop you. Enjoy it. Be you)*
> Food is love. *(Food is not love, but it is often used as a substitute for love)*

By the time you have looked through these stories and sayings, I think you will start to have an idea of where you are with your thinking and feelings. It is greatly beneficial for you to know you are not alone with your need for that extra food or weight and your feelings about yourself. All the clients I have quoted here or whose stories I have outlined, have lost weight because they have explored and understood why they have been overeating.

The aim of your journey is to discover what food and size mean for you and to make new decisions as each of these clients has done.

Part II

Your unique psychological journey towards understanding and weight loss

Chapter 7

Looking at your ways of being and doing: The Parent, Adult and Child in you

In my school of psychotherapy (Transactional Analysis or TA), we recognise there are three basic ways of being in the world. So that we can investigate triggers that lead you to overeat or be the unwanted size you are, I want to introduce you to these parts of yourself and show you how they operate. You will find that I refer to these parts of yourself in various ways as you work through the book. The idea is that you understand and use them too.

There are three different "parts" of the self with different ways of thinking, feeling and behaving. These are known as the "Parent ego-state", or the Parent self; The "Adult ego-state" or the Adult self and the "Child ego-state" or the Child self. Each part has a recognisable way of thinking, being and behaving. In our first level of enquiry, we consider the Parent ego-state to be the part that we have internalised from our actual parents and other parental figures. We copy their thoughts, feelings and behaviours and we can come to recognise when we are doing this. The Child ego-state replicates our thoughts feelings and behaviours from our childhood. With investigation, we can recognise when we are behaving, thinking or feeling as we did as a child. Our Adult self, or Adult ego-state, responds, thinks, feels and behaves in the here and now. When we are in our Adult ego-state we can observe our own behaviours, we can problem-solve, recognise our choices and make new decisions. You will note that we use capital letters for these ego-states to distinguish from actual parents, adults and children where we use lower case letters. So whenever you see Parent, Adult and Child with capitals, you will know we are discussing your inner-self and not actual people.

We draw these ego-states as three touching stacked circles. This shows (a) that they represent a whole self and (b) that there is a flow of energy between the ego-states. In other words, our energy can quickly move from Adult to Child or Parent. For example, we may be working in Adult when someone arrives with what feels like irresistible cream cakes. Our Adult may say that we don't want or need one, but the Child may feel deprived if we don't take one and will override the Adult and take a cake. We can also plot both our internal dialogues and our social interactions on these circles.

DOI: 10.4324/9781003240877-7

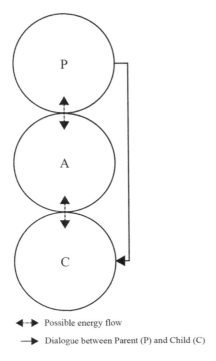

◀--▶   Possible energy flow

──▶   Dialogue between Parent (P) and Child (C)

Figure 7.1 Message from Parent to Child and possible energy flow between ego-states.

In Figure 7.1, I have drawn a simple transaction between the Inner Parent and Inner Child. The arrow comes from the Parent to the Child, so we know that there is a Parent message or direction to the Child. This is very significant when we are exploring why we overeat. We can draw arrows from any ego-state to any other ego-state to plot our internal voices. This helps us to see visually when we are in Child, Parent or Adult mode. All internal dialogue will use energy in Parent and Child when we are overeating and maintaining a larger body size than we want. When we investigate our behaviours and shift to new rational decisions in the present, we will be using our Adult.

When we are plotting a discussion or interchange with another person, we use two sets of three circles each with a Parent, Adult and Child representing the three ego-states of self and other. Our discussion can be shown to start with any one of the ego-states of one person to any ego-state of the other person (Figure 7.2).

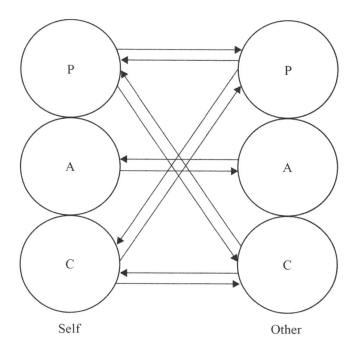

Self   Other

Figure 7.2 Possible communication channels between two sets of ego-states.

I have not drawn them all but there are 25 possible communication channels. As mentioned above, the two ego-states that are particularly concerned with overeating or maintaining a larger body size are the Child and the Parent. The Adult is used to understand and make new decisions and choices. For a little more information, we can divide the Child into

•   Natural Child (NC) who knows when we are hungry for food and knows when we have had enough, just as we did as infants. We would cry when hungry and let go of the breast or bottle when we had had enough.

    When you begin to distinguish the sensations that tell you when you are biologically hungry and when you have eaten enough food and don't need any more, you will have restored energy to the Natural Child within you.

    This ability to distinguish true biological hunger diminishes as we grow, because of the norms of society. For instance, we have times allotted to meals, i.e. breakfast, lunch, dinner. So we often eat when we might not be particularly hungry because there is work or school to attend to between those meal times. We can't normally eat just exactly when we want to. In such circumstances, we have adapted to the norms of our society and in doing so, lost some of those infant skills in knowing, through body sensation, when we are hungry and when satisfied. In later chapters, you will read about how you can regain this connection with your body self so that you can more clearly determine when you are hungry for food and when you are eating to satisfy an unconscious psychological need.

• Adapted Child (AC) who eats from an obedient place. The Adapted part of us obeys rules and directives given to us by significant others as children and beyond. Some rules are necessary and helpful and others unhelpful. As you progress through the book, you will come to see how you are still adapting to parental messages from your childhood. There are many other areas where we might continue to do as our parental figures told us but, here, we are concerned with those related to eating which are counter-productive for us. For instance, the idea that you eat everything and don't waste food would become "I must eat up and not waste food" in the Adapted Child. There is no Adult thinking that there might be times when it is better to leave food rather than to gather it on the body!

• The Rebellious Child (RC) eats from a place of rebelliousness. We are not always conscious of our rebellion, especially with regard to eating. The Rebellious Child often kicks against a diet or against a parental message or cultural message that says "slim is best". But it is generally more complex than this. If someone needs extra food or to be a larger size in the world and unconsciously fears being slim, then the Rebellious Child will ensure that any control of food intake does not last. This Rebellious Child aims to return to the familiar status quo of overeating. It may be this ego-state that leads you to sabotage your journey. This may well happen when underlying issues have not yet been resolved.

we can also divide the Parent Ego-State into:

• Controlling or Critical Parent (CP): Just as there is positive adaptation, there is good CP energy when there is constructive and affirmative guidance. However, when we look at how this ego-state persuades us to overeat, we can see that it is neither constructive nor affirmative. This ego-state often uses "shoulds" and "oughts", "musts" and "shouldn'ts" to control behaviour; Such as "you should go on a diet", "you shouldn't eat that". "you must have some more"; "you ought to think about people who haven't got much food, be grateful and finish what is on your plate." When we adapt to those sayings we are not using our Adult ego-state to make a decision. We just respond from an Adapted Child place to that Controlling Parent.

• Nurturing Parent (NP): Nurturing Parent can be helpful or disruptive. A positively nurturing self will be empathic and understanding, whilst a negative Nurturing Parent will unhelpfully suggest you have something to eat when you are upset. A negative Nurturing Parent will use food to compensate and soothe.

The Adult ego-state

The Ego-state that resolves the underlying issues that drive someone to overeat is the Adult self. We need the Adult, which is attuned to the here and now, to observe and understand what is happening. The Adult is the problem-solving ego-state. Rather than deciding to overeat, the Adult will find resolution so that eating in response to psychological needs is no longer necessary. Your Adult will guide you in making choices of what and when to eat. The Adult takes into consideration what the Child wants and the Parent demands and negotiates towards an appropriate conclusion.

In Transactional Analysis, we think of the ego-states as having energy which we then use in the ways described above. Because we have a fixed amount of energy to distribute amongst our ego-states it follows that if you have lots of energy in your Child and Parent there will be far less in your Adult. This is certainly the case when overeating is the issue. We need appropriately balanced energy in all our ego-states. In different circumstances, we may need to use one more than another. For instance, when in an office meeting or carrying out responsible duties, we would predominantly operate from our Adult selves. If we are playing with children, we might engage our Child selves but we would also need some Adult energy to ensure the play is safe.

So, for us to move towards eating less and losing weight, we need to increase the energy and strength of the Adult. We need to consider what is going on using Adult reasoning and objectivity. If you are overweight and don't want to be, then your Child is orchestrating it for a reason. Once you realise what forces are behind your overeating, you can use your Adult self to make sense of them, understand them and find ways to resolve them and make changes. Your positive Nurturing Parent will help you by being patient and considerate; by encouraging and being supportive.

Just reading through this book and working on the exercises will increase the strength of your Adult because much of the time you will be investigating your thoughts feelings and behaviours around food, learning about yourself and reflecting on your answers. All this takes Adult energy.

If we sneak food whilst no one is looking, keep food in the car "just in case....", when we continue eating until we feel bloated, when we treat ourselves to extra pudding even though we are full, finish a cake because there is only one slice left, when we succumb to the invitation to be "naughty" and have something scrumptious that we don't really want or agree to eat more because someone says "why won't you have more, don't you like it?", we are in our Child ego-state. Knowing this helps us to choose another ego-state to deal with these situations. This would primarily be the Adult self, alongside a caring and understanding Nurturing Parent self. In a way, the Adult can choose the ego-state we employ at any one time.

When in the Parent ego-state we respond in ways that we learnt from parents and significant parental figures in our lives. There will be times when we can hear in our heads a message from our actual parent figures and it is good to recognise these with regard to eating. For instance, the directive to "finish the food on your plate", sometimes accompanied by phrases like "think of the starving millions" or a threat like "or you'll have no pudding" is readily identifiable as something a parent actually says. You can still here the voices that said it. So often this rule is so embedded in the psyche of our grown-up selves that we continue to obey it without recognising what and why we are doing it and without further thought. We are hardly aware that the Parent in us is repeating the demand and the Child within us is obeying. Until we start to focus on these internal voices or dialogues, we are unaware of how we are still obeying others' rules.

Focussing on your eating, do you find yourself finishing everything on your plate, ignoring the fact that you are feeling full? Do you think that you cannot have a pudding if you haven't eaten your entire main course? If you reflect a bit more, can you hear, in your head, someone telling you to do this? If you can hear that voice, can you identify whose it is? It may not be one of your actual parents, but some other influence in your life. We receive these messages, from other parent influences such as grandparents, aunts, uncles, older siblings or teachers and many more. So you might identify someone other than your actual parents.

If you lose weight through negative Parent forces and Child adaptations, you will invariably not maintain those losses. All steps to lose weight need to have a conscious Adult input in order to be permanent. When in the Adult ego-state, we are in the present: thinking, feeling, deciding and behaving in an appropriate and resourceful grown-up way. The Adult is the problem-solving ego-state. The Adult enables us to make considered choices. It is the part of us that ultimately works out why we are overweight when we don't want to be. The Adult can observe and respond with reasoning; can work things out; can intervene in the dialogue between the Child and Parent that leads to overeating.

Now use your Adult to look at the common command of finishing everything on your plate. I use this command and similar examples throughout the book but you will have your own family sayings and directives that you will identify and use instead, later in this chapter.

Would you, as your grown-up self, still think it is necessary to eat everything on your plate even if you have had enough of that food?

If you ask yourself "Why?" you should not leave food on your plate and your reply is, for instance, that "you musn't waste food", you are not in your Adult. What is more wasteful or inappropriate than forcing down the food you don't want, letting some of that collect on your body, and eliminating the rest down the loo? Better to leave it, compost it, recycle it, give it to your pet or just throw it away. Why be the go-between from your plate to the toilet when you can put it down the toilet without it having to go through your body and leave its negative deposits on the way? " This is Adult thinking.

And now consider this type of dictate: you can't have pudding until you have eaten everything on your plate. Is it actually necessary to eat it up so that you can have a pudding?

What is the rationale for doing this? Does it make sense?

It might just be that you have had enough of one set of flavours and are ready to change to something else. Finishing what you do not want for some obscure reason, is part of overeating. It is unnecessary and your Adult will tell you so and your Child will change when s/he is ready to hear and accept it.

Your Adult will tell you that you do not have to obey these old rules because you are old enough to make up your own mind and weigh up the pros and cons. Your Adult will tell you that you can make your own new decisions and corresponding choices.

Let's look at another everyday thing your parents might have said. Again, I will suggest a simple example and then you can add and consider your own. "I made this especially for you". With the unspoken words that indicate you must have some and/or some more. The unspoken, yet implied, words are the psychological message. It is implied by tones and facial expressions, and maybe gestures. From the unspoken, your Child gets the message that you cannot refuse and have no choice but to eat because someone has made it especially for you.

This may appear to be tricky when you are physically with the person who has made whatever food it is and wants you to eat it. The invitation is to eat it whether you want it or not. It holds a guilt-making message. You do have to be strong and in your Adult to refuse this food. Just as the person wanting you to eat enforces the invitation by tones, (e.g. pleading) facial expressions that say "please don't refuse me" and gestures such as holding the plate of food under your nose, you need to look and sound like you are in your Adult ego-state. Your message will then transmit as respectful and decisive.

A process of investigation for you with your Adult energy, which will only take a second, is:

- **Do I want this food? If not why would I eat it?**
- **Do I need to please this other person, whoever s/he is? Why would I do that?**

- Listen to your answers and then make an appropriate decision.
- Feel yourself in your Adult and find the adult words to respond.

My examples for exploration might not be those in your experience but they serve to show you how you can counteract outdated parental orders with questions from your Adult ego-state.

The following exercise guides you to recognise and work through your family sayings.

Exercise I   Your family sayings

1. Write down five sayings about food and eating that you recall from your childhood.

2. Reflect on how these operate in your life now and jot down what you notice.

Changing your message

1. Write down one of your own messages about eating or food that you would like to change.

2. From your Adult ask yourself why this is a rule you have continued to follow.

3. Then: Is it valid and rational to obey this now I am a grown-up?

4. Why?

5. Wait for a moment. Do you feel any agitation now? if yes, your Child self is responding to the idea of change. You can reassure your Child that it is OK to continue, or you may want to stop and come back to this question later.

6. If you can, make your new decision: From now on I will:

7. My Adult self says it is fine to do this for myself now because:

You can use this exercise as many times as you find yourself obeying someone else's rules or being persuaded to eat when you don't really want to.

You are in charge of your eating and your well-being. This is a powerful way to be. Why would anyone else have the right to "make you do" something you don't want to do? Remember that no one, in normal circumstances, can make you do anything. As a grown-up, you always have a choice. You have the final say as an equal.

In this exercise, you notice I ask whether you feel any agitation as you answered the questions. I ask because it might be that your Child self becomes agitated at the thought of doing what you want to do rather than obeying someone else's rule. In the next chapter, we will look at the reasons for this agitation. For now, be interested in all your thoughts and feelings as they are giving you important information. It might help you to make a note of them too.

When you are with someone who is tempting you to eat you might like to arm yourself with Adult responses such as: "I really appreciated that, but I can't eat anything else now". "I enjoyed what I had but don't want any more". The aim is to stay in your Adult self. If you waver, your Internal Controlling Parent will tell you that you *should* eat it and your Child will obey!

There are two different scenarios to consider here. One is when we are physically involved with others who try to influence our eating; the other is when we hear those same messages in our heads.

Hearing old orders in our heads

The initial process of questioning remains the same whether you are with someone who lures you into eating extra food or whether your internal Parent is doing the luring. Here we are examining the messages in your head. It is a new skill to stop and question why you are going to eat extra food in either case and it is a skill you will learn to use gradually as you progress. You only need to take a very short time to stop for a moment and ask yourself those same edifying questions. Pausing for a moment to think in your Adult is key. In that pause, you can reflect on who would have "planted" those messages in your psyche. For instance, if you find yourself obeying the edict of eating everything on your plate, then stop and go through those questions of Why? Does it make sense? Where does it come from? And so forth. You can then decide whether to obey or not.

Don't be discouraged if you continue to eat it all up. This is a step by step journey. It is helpful to think in this way: If you make sure you at least stop for a moment, you are already in a new way of being. You may be able to sense that your Inner Child is obeying an old rule and it may be s/he feels agitated about doing anything else. Your Nurturing Parent can be compassionate and your Adult might say "go ahead, it's OK, we can find out later why you feel agitated". You give yourself "permission" which takes you away from automatically obeying past rules towards actually making a decision on your own behalf here and now.

If questioning does make you feel anxious or agitated, be curious as to why you are feeling this agitation. It tells you that there is more to be explored before you can change this action. This is very useful to know. You may not be ready to change until you have done this further exploration.

If you are ready, look at Exercise 2.

Exercise 2   Being tempted by others

Think of a time recently when you have been lured into eating by someone else.
1. Who was with you at the time?

2. How did they lure you into eating more than you wanted?

3. What words did they use?

4. How did you feel when they encouraged you to eat more?

5. Did you comply by eating more?

6. If your answer is "yes" to the above question, why do you think you complied against your will?

7. How did you feel after you had eaten it?

8. What might you have done differently?

Exercise 3   Familiar messages in your head

Now let us review a time when you have obeyed an old message in your head.

1. How did the voice in your head lure you into eating more than you wanted?

2. What words did you hear?

3. Who do you recognise as having said this? Whose voice is it?

4. Why is this voice so strong or compelling?

5. How did you feel when the old message encouraged you to eat more?

6. Did you comply by eating more?

7. Why do you think you complied against your will?

8. How did you feel after you had eaten it?

9. As this is a voice in your head, do you think you might be able to do something different next time?

---

10. What choices do you have in future?

Let us now look at the pattern of yoyo (on and off and on and off) dieting in terms of your ego-states.

Ego-state explanation of the "on-off," or yo-yo, diet cycle

The cycle of overeating, gaining weight, dieting, then overeating (yo-yo dieting) involves the Parent and Adapted Child ego-states. We know that there are people who will actually tell you to diet, but we also know we can tell ourselves in the same way. Our internal Critical Parent will use the same kinds of words: "You should diet and lose weight", though often when we say this to ourselves it is accompanied by unkind self-deprecation. The Adapted Child within us will obey both others, strong cultural messages and our own psychological messages. This explanation of yo-yo dieting includes the point at which you stop the diet. If you are eating for psychological reasons then those reasons will become more powerful if you deprive yourself of the food that has been used as an attempt to resolve or diminish the painful feelings involved. The Child self, who is dependent on overeating and/or a larger body size, will not be able to tolerate the reduction in food for very long. It will feel like being deprived, and the Child becomes fearful. Look at the dialogues below. The Critical Parent might be a real person, the message in your own head or even cultural persuasions. For clarity, the related diagrams follow.

Critical Parent: "You are overweight, you **should** diet"
Adapted Child: I **must** diet.

After some time in a restrictive regime, the whole thing becomes too much because food is needed as an attempt to avoid facing psychological hungers, and so the Rebellious Child kicks back to regain the status quo; i.e. overeating. This position will be familiar and therefore feel safer.

Rebellious Child: I've had enough dieting and I am going to eat **whatever I want**.

This is what it looks like in our three-circle diagram (Figure 7.3): The diet-eat cycle.

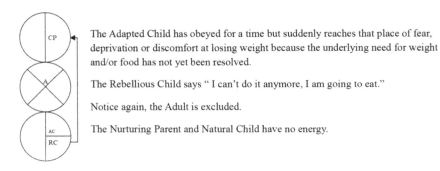

The Critical Parent to the Adapted Child:

"You must diet, you're overweight".

The Adapted Child to the Critical Parent:

"I must diet, and lose weight"

The Adapted Child has obeyed. Notice that the Adult is excluded and has no say in this dialogue. There is no energy in the Nurturing Parent or Natural Child.

The Adapted Child has obeyed for a time but suddenly reaches that place of fear, deprivation or discomfort at losing weight because the underlying need for weight and/or food has not yet been resolved.

The Rebellious Child says " I can't do it anymore, I am going to eat."

Notice again, the Adult is excluded.

The Nurturing Parent and Natural Child have no energy.

Figure 7.3 The diet-eat cycle.

It might be that you have actually heard the words "You should diet because you are overweight" from someone around you, or indeed surmised it from attitudes in our culture. Or it might be that you have internalised this message for yourself, such that now and again it pops up in your Parent self and you obey from your Child self. If you are not ready to lose that weight, you are very likely going to hit that place where it seems impossible to continue. In this instance, the Rebellious Child is refusing to continue the weight loss regime because it is frightening to do so when food or weight has been used as a "protection" against, as yet, undiscovered psychological issues or needs.

If you recognise this pattern, there are a number of ways of helping yourself to break this cycle.

*   Be curious about your feelings and what has happened.
*   Unlock your Adult self. Try to get into your Adult by straightening your posture, moving to a space where you are most likely to be in your Adult self such as a study or a chair at a desk where you work in your

Adult; Sometimes just standing straight with your head held high, taking a good deep breath or sitting upright in a certain chair that is not where you relax, will enable you to feel Adult energy. Practise speaking out loud in a grown-up voice. Listen to and aim to negotiate with your Child and Parent ego-states

- Aim to pinpoint the moment when you rebelled against your inner Critical Parent. What happened? What did you really need? Use the chapters in this book to help you discover what underlying and unconscious needs you may be missing.
- If you can, aim to think about normal and healthy foods rather than a fixed regime diet. Gradually change your foods. Not everyone can eat the same things, so you need to find what foods are right for you in, taste, texture and colour, for your enjoyment. It is also true that different foods will put weight on for one person but not for the next. Aim to reduce the amount of food on your plate, little by little.
- Use any feeling of agitation that might lead you to overeat as important information. As we know you are worth this effort, treat every sensation, feeling, emotion, behavioural change as indications of something you need to know and that your body and unconscious selves are telling you something very significant. Make a note of these feelings and behaviours.
- This sensitive and understanding approach will help to avoid that place of fear, discomfort or sense of deprivation.
- Be compassionate towards yourself. Remember you only ever resume your journey from where you left off. There is no failure. You just continue when ready and move forwards.
- If this seems too much to do on your own, seek counselling or psychotherapeutic help, using this book as a basis for discussion.

The yo-yo pattern of losing weight, gaining, losing, gaining, is likely to be repeated and repeated until the related underlying issues have been resolved and the Adult self is activated. If you have followed many diets over the years, then you have most likely been locked in this pattern of eating. Your Adult is the part of you that decides and chooses to lose weight, sensibly and gradually, using healthy normal foods and no fad diets or directed eating. As you have seen so far, your Adult self is usually excluded in this process such that Critical Parent and Adapted Child and then Rebellious Child can just continue without Adult guidance.

Let's look a little deeper as to why your Rebellious Child might stop the diet. There are a number of reasons and these may relate to the self-sabotage you identified in chapter 5.

First, as we have already discovered, if there are psychological reasons why we overeat, and these unconscious motives have not been addressed and resolved, the Child will need to stick to being overweight and overeating; hence the Rebellious side of the Child will intervene and stop the diet.

Second, if part of the problem is that the Child believes that you need to be big in the world in order to feel safe or to cope with burdens of life, or imagines that extending the body boundary keeps people at a distance, then once again the Rebellious Child will rebel and refuse to diet any longer. She/ he will not be willing to lose the protective armour she/he has gathered around the body self.

Third, the Child becomes fearful of losing the prop of food that she/he believes has kept him/her safe somehow, or met a need that has not been explored and resolved. We know that overeating does not resolve underlying psychological needs but we can, and need to, know this in all our ego-states and let our Adult selves work with us. With the resolution of these psychological needs, the Child becomes calmer. Calming the Child allows a gap in which to insert Adult thinking and reflection.

So, for us to move towards eating less and losing weight we need to increase the energy and strength of the Adult. We need to consider what is going on using Adult reasoning and objectivity. Child fears are persuasive. For instance, fear of there not being enough food, which might seem strange on the surface, but is a remarkably familiar belief; as are beliefs of not being good enough and feelings of being alone, abandoned or under-stimulated. I have often found that feelings of being unloved or even unlovable have been existential beliefs behind the need for extra food. In the next chapter, you will investigate more of your own such unhelpful beliefs that push you to overeat.

As previously described, we use our ego-states differently in differing circumstances. So someone with a demanding job that needs quick and evaluative thinking skills will use a lot of Adult when at work. But, just because someone has a demanding Adult job does not mean that they will remain in their Adult when leaving work or that they can maintain that Adult around eating if there are underlying issues that need to be brought into awareness.

The Child in us really has very potent energy and it is that energy you feel when you have a strong urge to eat and feel you cannot resist. Such energy is strong enough to decommission both the Adult and the Parent if eating or maintaining weight feels necessary or even, at times, like a survival issue. This is why it is so important to aim to pause for a second or two before eating, with the promise that the Child can still have that food. Pausing before eating is a very important part of your journey. It allows for energy to flow to the Adult which means we can start in that moment of pausing, to look at what forces are driving us to overeat.

By responding to the questions listed 1–3, you began to bring into awareness messages common in your family around eating. These concerned a recognisable Controlling Parent message, your Adapted Child response and an introduction to Adult evaluation and invitation to do things differently. The following questions help you to examine your behaviour in more specific contexts. They enable you to see how you can be dragged back into family and familiar environments and revert to old thinking and obeying just by being with someone who was a major figure in your childhood.

Imagine you are going to visit your parents or someone else who may have been influential in your development. Grandparents, aunts, school teachers, club leaders, even neighbours, can fall into this category if they have influenced, guided (or misguided) you. These can all be seen as parent figures. The thoughts, feelings, beliefs and behaviours of these parent types become the integrated Parent within your Parent self and continue to influence in the same way. So let's start by looking at these parental influences. Write down your answer to the questions.

The first scenes relate to physically being with (1) female influences and (2) male influences. The third scene is you in your own home.

Try to write down what you are feeling as you read and respond to these questions. Just a few brief words will do, e.g. agitated, angry, sad, happy, confused etc. or sum up your feelings at the end of each scene.

Before you start, recap or write down five sayings common in your childhood home around eating, food, weight and mealtimes. This time, write who said them alongside each one.

1.

2.

3.

4.

5.

Scene 1 Imagine you are with the Female influences from your childhood, e.g. mother, grandmother, aunt, sister, etc.

Imagine the scene clearly and watch your behaviour in your mind's eye or watch it on an imaginary screen in front of you. Take time to really look at what happens. We often revert back to some part of the childhood relationship when we are with influential others, especially in their homes.

1. In your scene, who are you with?

2. Do you change your behaviour when with this person? If so, how?

3. Do you feel like you become a child again in the relationship? What is it you are aware of that you do or don't do?

4. Do you find yourself being timid, holding back on things you would otherwise be free to say, or do? (Add a few notes here)

5. Think for a moment about the differences in yourself that you are aware of in this scene and write down some related words.

6. When you eat together, do you eat what she wants you to eat whether you want to or not?

7. Are you drawn in to eat something you don't want to by the other person's persuasive language or tones? E.g. "go on, just a little bit", "for me" or "I cooked this for you", or a sense of being rebelliously playful together because of sharing something "naughty but nice"? Which of your five sayings comes to mind? Can you say why?

8. In your imagined scene are you doing what you want to do?

9. If you find yourself behaving like the child in these relationships, especially around eating and mealtimes, write down why you think this is.

10. Finally, does it make sense to continue to obey these types of demands in your own life now? Write down why not.

What do you notice about what you have written in this section? Jot down a few words.

Scene 2   You are now with the male influences in your life: father, uncle, grandfather etc. Answer the same questions with regard to male influences from your child-hood and write your answers below.

(Again, try to write down what you are feeling as you read and respond to these questions. Just a few brief words will do e.g. agitated, angry, sad, happy, confused etc. or you can do this at the end, whichever is right for you.)

Imagine the scene clearly and watch your behaviour in your mind's eye. Take time to really look at what happens.

1. In your scene, who are you with?

2. Do you change your behaviour when with this person? If so, how?

3. Do you feel like you become a child again in the relationship? What is it you are aware of that you do or don't do?

4. Do you find yourself being timid, holding back on things you would otherwise be free to say, or do? (Add a few notes here)

5. Think for a moment about the differences in yourself that you are aware of in this scene and write down some related words.

6. When you eat together, do you eat what he wants you to eat whether you want to or not?

7. Are you drawn in to eat something you don't want to by the other person's persuasive language or tones? E.g. "go on, just a little bit", "for me" or "I don't want to eat alone" ", or a sense of being rebelliously playful together because of sharing something "naughty but nice"? Which of your own five sayings comes to mind? Can you say why?

8. In your imagined scene are you doing what <u>you</u> want to do?

9. If you find yourself behaving like the child in these relationships, especially around eating and mealtimes, write down why you think this is.

10. Finally, does it make sense to continue to obey these types of demands in your own life now? Write down why not.

What do you notice about what you have written in this section? Jot down a few words.

A. How does your list of five sayings about eating, food, mealtimes, and weight help you to see what happens to you around food?

B. What do you notice about the answers you have given to each of these sets of questions? Is there a difference in your thoughts, feelings and behaviours when thinking about male or female influences? Write down a few observations.

Now in your own environment

1. Reflect on your own behaviour, thoughts and feelings around mealtimes, food and eating now in your grown-up life. Go back through your answers above and write down what you are still believing, obeying and even passing on to your own children in your own home.

2. Whose are the main voices you hear around eating and size?

3. Now that you are aware of whose voices you hear compelling you to eat, what might you say to them, here and now, as your grown-up self?

4. As you say your words above to those voices, what will you say to yourself?

5.   Why is this helpful to you?

6.   Now when you eat, whether at mealtimes or any other time of day, aim to bring some of these messages and your answers into your head.

It really is interesting that we will continue with old ways that have been instilled in us from childhood, whether we are with parent figures or not. Like clearing your plate even if you are full. We can even eat meals that are familiar from our childhood without thinking about alternatives, or we can eat in front of the TV because that is what we have always done; Or we might rebel and eat in front of the TV because that was not allowed when we were children. It doesn't matter what the scenario is, if we do not want to do the same things anymore, we need to know exactly what we are doing, and why, so that we can do something different. We can give ourselves permission to do what we want to do as grown-ups. It is important to see where we might be carrying on with behaviours from the past that we don't want to do anymore and the questions you have just answered will have thrown some light on this for you.

It is not possible for me to include all situations in which you might find yourself adapting to others whether those people are from your childhood, others in your past or in the present. I hope that these exercises help to awaken your awareness of what is happening at an otherwise unaware level. They bring the unconscious into your consciousness.

Your internal discussions, i.e. The dialogue that occurs between your Inner Child and Parent ego-states.

If you think about your answers again, you may be able to recognise an internal discussion or dialogue that goes on. Maybe you will recognise a struggle in your head between your internal ego-states . For instance:

Adult:	"I don't want that cake,
Adapted Child:	if I don't eat it mum/dad/friend will be cross/unhappy, think I am ungrateful".
Adult:	"I really don't want to stay for dinner tonight"
Adapted Child :	but s/he has cooked it and it would be rude and inconsiderate not to stay. Mum would get upset and Dad would think I don't love him".

Let's look at some ways in which you can recognise and change your internal dialogue so you can do what is right for you. I will give the examples that we have looked at before. These scenarios are templates for your own investigation. You can substitute what you heard and received as a child and look at how you can counteract some of those messages now.

Remember what we hear and receive as kids from actual other people gets internalised into our own mind and becomes part of our own internal dialogue too.

What we are looking at here are sayings that we can locate and remember from others who we can identify. We are also looking at psychological messages accompanying these words. The psychological messages are most persuasive.

The recommended alternative Adult responses can be used both towards another who is present in the here and now, or towards the messages that go round in your own head when the other person isn't present.

When you get used to this idea, you will feel that sense of choice that I introduced earlier. It only takes a brief second to connect with your Adult self, once you get used to feeling his/her presence. So, to pause for a moment is a particularly good and powerful idea. This pause is potent, whether you are physically with another person who "makes you eat" or whether you are thinking about your own internal dialogue.

For each of the proposed messages that follow, write down who said this to you and your Adapted Child response and then add in your Adult response.

Keep in your Adult with Adult words and minimal, concise replies. The Adult does not use excuses.

Parent message	Adapted Child	Adult alternative
1. "Finish everything on your plate."	"I must eat it all"	"I've had enough now"
2. "You are staying for dinner aren't You?	I don't want to but must	(your answer)
3. "Have a bit more cake. I made it for you. It will go to waste if you don't eat it"	(your answer here)	(your answer)
4. Your message here.	(your answer here)	(your answer)
5. Your message here.	(your answer here)	(your answer)
6. Your message here.	(your answer here)	(your answer)

If, in reality, the other person tries to persuade you, you just repeat the same Adult words. Even if we have to say it three or four times, the other person will eventually catch on that your Adapted Child is not playing ball and your Adult is saying "no thanks".

Repeating your Adult response will strengthen you and your resolve as well as convince the other person you won't be persuaded to do otherwise.

The psychological message

With many of the sayings around food and eating, there are unspoken inferences. These are psychological or ulterior messages and as I have said before can be very persuasive. Frequently around food, eating and weight they are aimed at raising guilt feelings. For example, the message "eat everything on your plate" is often accompanied by: "There are children in the world who don't have food". The psychological message is "how come you can leave food when there are children starving?" or "You should be grateful you have food on your plate", in other words, "you are ungrateful". Once guilt is experienced it becomes a persuasive emotion to do as asked. The psychological message inducing guilt might not be in words but in gestures or tones. e.g. the sad, hurt look when you don't want seconds, or you don't want to stay for dinner, or you won't have more cake. These psychological messages are extremely potent. The psychological messages, in this context, are almost always from Parent to Child.

When you consider your own recognised messages, try to find the unspoken luring psychological messages. You can do this by thinking about what you experience physically and the dialogue that goes on in your mind. Use the examples above to help you write below what you discover.

Reaffirming your Adult

Answer "Yes" or "No" to these questions to connect with your Adult:

1. **Are you an adult in your own right, with responsibilities and decision-making capacities?**
2. **Have you got a job that involves thinking for yourself?**
3. **Do you look after children and/or others who need you to be rational and in control?**
4. **Do you have to make important decisions regularly?**
5. **Do you have to travel, drive, shop, manage finances?**

Thinking with your Adult ego-state: Are there really any reasons that mean you are required to be an Adapted Child around eating? What is the worst thing that could happen if you use your Adult?

Go back through the questions where you imagined times when you are with or visit the male and female influence/parental figures from your childhood.

Feeling the strength of your Adult, what will you now say?

In conclusion: There follow points that will help you to use the information you have gathered so far. They are points to which you will refer again in other chapters and exercises.

1. Always take your time. Give a little pause before you respond. It only needs a second to get to know what you are feeling and what you really want to do.
2. As you are pausing be aware of what is going on in your body.
3. Check if you are feeling comfortable in your body.
4. Check if you feel some agitation, or butterflies, or any discomfort.
5. Checking with your body self will indicate if there is something not quite right. It can help you know that you are being asked to do something you don't want to do and then you can use your Adult to acknowledge that it is reasonable not to want to do it. There are exercises in chapter 11 to guide you as to how to be in touch with body sensations if the scenario you are in seems difficult.
6. Pause and listen to the words in your head. If you are being asked (or are asking yourself) to do something that deep down you don't want to do, it will be clear from the words in your head. You will hear yourself go through the arguments such as "I don't want that" and then the other side saying "yes you do, go on, it won't hurt". Or "I don't want that" and the other side saying: "but I must eat it because...."
7. Aim to relax, take a breath, stand or sit up straight and let your Adult think about this. Why would you accept to do something, maybe eat something, you really don't want?
8. Aim to ask yourself: "What does my Adult say?"
9. With practice, your Adult will be able to say: "I am a grown up now and I can make my own choices and decisions according to what is right for me". "I do not have to please anyone else when I know it is not right for me to do something."

I have endeavoured to explain the ego-state system as simply as possible as a starting point to get to know the available parts of yourself and how they influence your eating and weight. When we can hear the words spoken by authority figures in our lives, we can consider them and see if they fit for us as the autonomous grown-ups we now are.

This chapter has focussed on recognition of things that have actually been said to us and using our Adult ego-state to make different choices. This will work for you unless you find that it starts to raise agitated feelings. This will probably mean that there is something deeper going on. In the next chapter, we look at what might be happening in the unconscious that is causing this agitation.

Chapter 8

Further focus on how your Child self can influence your eating and weight

In the last chapter, I demonstrated how your Parent and Child selves influence your eating and weight and how your Adult can resolve issues once they are brought into awareness.

In this chapter, I focus on the conclusions we make from our experiences in the world from birth and throughout childhood that affect our sense of self and influence our choices regarding eating and weight. These are decisions made early in our lives without the presence of a developed Adult ego-state. In other words, we make some decisions from the experiences we have and sensations we encounter around others without the ability to test our understanding of what is happening.

It might be that the investigations in chapter 7 lead to a positive and satisfactory shift in behaviour but it might also be that it is not yet the full story. Recognising underlying influences enables us to dispel the power that keeps the Adapted Child adapted. It is intriguing and exciting. Do not worry if there are bits that you don't understand, you can still work through the questions which will help you make sense of it all. If, however, in reading this information and working through the exercises you start to feel fearful or agitated to a point that seems unmanageable, I strongly suggest you seek therapeutic help and work on this level of self-exploration with your therapist, using this book for refernce.

Whereas many of our experiences in life have been understood with some Adult energy available to think about them, in early years there is no developed Adult to make sense of the world, so, in a way, we use sensation and intuition to form conclusions. These conclusions are often erroneous such that we can live our lives believing something that is not true. These decisions affect our sense of self and can influence our choices regarding eating and weight.

As outlined in chapter 7, we can recognise voices in our head that direct us with regard to many of our behaviours around food and eating, however,

DOI: 10.4324/9781003240877-8

the self-concluded messages we are exploring here tend not to be so obvious in their origin. We don't recognise who said them because the words themselves have never actually been said. We have made our deductions from our sense of what is going on or have misinterpreted the meaning of words, emotions and behaviours of others around us. Because we are unable to rationalise our experiences, thoughts and feelings, some of our conclusions can seem quite bizarre.

I wrote briefly about Rowena's story in chapter 6. Rowena never knew her mother as she died when Rowena was a baby. She didn't experience a mother's attunement and mirroring, holding, warmth and love that are so needed in infancy. Rowena's infant mind needed to find a reason for her mother's absence. She could have decided that mother was bad as she had left her but this would have been even more painful than blaming herself for what happened. She, therefore, concluded that she was herself to blame for her mother's absence and in so doing decided that she (Rowena) was not lovable hence her mother left. Because her father never talked to her about her mother's life or death, she maintained that belief until, in her early forties, she came into therapy to work with her weight issues. It was in therapy that she discovered her infant conclusion of being unlovable and understood how she had, without evidence, made this unreal conclusion. She re-decided that her mother did love her and that she was lovable. This was a clear turning point in her journey.

Rowena's story is complex. There were many layers to address in therapy until we reached her core belief which was that her mother didn't love her and therefore died. Let's look briefly at the layers of life events that caused Rowena to overeat.

Rowena had concluded that her mother didn't love her and so left her, and as a consequence decided that she herself must be unlovable. Furthermore, she construed that if she was unlovable, she must be "bad". Her large body size, therefore, also had the illusionary function of "hiding" her bad self.

Rowena craved the maternal love she missed and ate to feed the yearning.

Being a child without a mother, she carried more responsibilities than were appropriate for her age. She felt she needed to be "a big girl". This is a phrase often used to control children's emotions and behaviour. This conscious decision is often unconsciously interpreted as needing to be big physically. This leads to overeating in order to produce the "protective" armour which is the fat around the body that becomes the large size.

Rowena's was perhaps a bizarre conclusion. There had been no words spoken that told her she was unlovable. This is an example of how the infant deals psychologically with experiences and how the Child self operates in an attempt to make sense of the world around them.

Though these beliefs are in response to parental figures, we don't hear the direct words of those people in our heads. They are messages unconsciously conjured up by the Child in order to negotiate the world around them. They are interpretations of what adults and other influential people are doing and saying and are constructed stories about ourselves from birth onwards. When they are self-created like this we can consider them as being "lodged" in the Child ego-state.

We often have a vague sense of these erroneous conclusions although, until we consider them, they do not appear to us to be wrong. For instance, I have heard people say things like "I don't deserve to be happy" or "I am not worthwhile" inside and outside the therapy room. When we stop to think about them we can recognise that they are ideas that have arisen through misunderstandings and misinterpretations, usually in childhood. At an existential level, at the core of ourselves, we all have a right to happiness and to feel that we are worthwhile as human beings and individuals in the world. Whoever said that life needs to be miserable? Who can ever say that someone is not worthwhile? These constructs are within ourselves. We have made them. Hence the mantras I suggested you repeat for yourself: "I am OK"; "I can think"; "I can decide for myself and choose" and "I am worth it." They all make sense as a basis for our humanity. When we stray from believing them we need to discover why.

I do not wish to delve too deeply into this level of unconscious beliefs as in some instances this can cause agitation and, as I have said before, could become overwhelming. However, what we can do here is to maintain our Adult observer and thinking selves and be curious about these core beliefs and how they might arise and affect our eating and body size.

In TA we recognise different ways in which the Child ego-state "operates". As the focus of this book is not TA theory, I am going to outline the different processes as simply as I can which may mean using slightly different terminology to that used in pure TA.

The different parts of the Child that are of particular interest to us are what we call the Parent in the Child and the Child in the Child ego-state. For ease of understanding, I am going to call the Parent in the Child the "Young Parent" in order to distinguish it from the Parent described in the last chapter and I will use the words "Child in the Child" as this is the best description. Here is what this looks like diagrammatically (Figure 8.1).

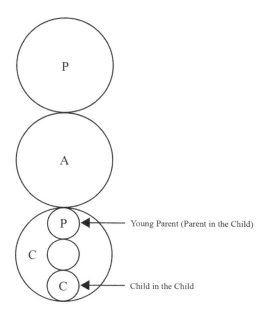

Figure 8.1 The Parent and Child in the Child ego-state.

Let's now look at each of these parts of the Child in a little more depth and see how they influence eating patterns.

Young Parent (Parent in the Child)

The young Parent will invent ways of coping with the world around him or her in order to get needs met or to protect against perceived threats. These "threats" can be something like parents' anger or disappointment. Even these situations that are manageable later in life can be construed by the youngster as leading to something more severe such as being abandoned or unloved. In this way, the Young Parent creates ways of keeping him or herself in line with what is expected of them, i.e. to obey the rules.

Let's take the message we have looked at in some depth in other chapters: "Eat everything on your plate." If I, as a youngster, don't want to do this but must obey the rule, I might decide to make sense of it by creating the belief that something dreadful will happen if I refuse. After all, there is not usually a verifiable reason for finishing everything on the plate. So as children, we unconsciously make up a reason for needing to obey the rule, such as, "I will starve if I don't eat up", or "mum won't love me if I don't obey", or even, "they will abandon me". These are ways in which the Young Parent convinces the Child in the Child it must obey. In a way, it frightens itself into complying. These thoughts that lead to obeying the rules remain in the unconscious such that we find ourselves, as adults, doing things without question until we bring them into consciousness and confront them. So if you are someone who was told this message when young, you may have, in your unconscious, construed a reason for it needing to be obeyed. Did your parent tell you a good reason why you should "eat up" that convinced you that you should always do so? Most likely, at an unconscious level, you made up a reason yourself, along the lines of those suggested above.

Basically, in order to make sense of things and ensure compliance, we will make up a reason that is strong enough to dismiss any ideas of disobeying. The Young Parent takes care of this.

We also looked at those alluring invitations to eat when we wouldn't want to even as adults. When someone entices you to eat because they have "prepared it just for you", or want you to join in the suggested naughtiness of sharing a lovely looking cream cake, why is it so difficult at times to say no? My work has so often revealed that, deep down, there is a Child influence that believes that the other person won't like or love them if they refuse. You can see the Young Parent scaring the child into obeying, i.e. eating the food regardless, by saying "They won't love you if you don't eat that food ." Or "You'll never get asked round for tea again". We know from the last chapter that the Adapted Child obeys but what drives the Adapted Child to obey can be this sort of self-regulatory uncomfortable or frightening message.

Another way in which the Young Parent creates instructions is by interpreting the behaviour of the adults. For instance, if a parent is too busy to respond to or play with a son or daughter, they may decide that they are not important enough to warrant their parent's attention. So an order of "Don't be important" will filter into the Parent in the Child. Two therapists, Bob and Mary Goulding,[1] found that there are twelve themes that arise when considering these negative decisions made in childhood. They called these "injunctions" and I see them as being held in the Young Parent.

These are non-verbal, unconscious communications from significant other people, usually parents and caregivers. They all start with "Don't". Remember they are normally not verbal messages from parental figures, they are what we as kids interpret from the parental behaviours. I briefly describe five of these themes, known as injunctions, so that you can see how they contribute to overeating and being overweight. After each description, I include a related exercise.

"Don't be important". When children are ignored or put down they start to believe they are not important. This injunction keeps people from reaching the goals to which they aspire which gives rise to frustration. It can be interpreted in a number of ways such as "I am not good enough to be important" which leads to a lack of self-worth or "I must not ask for what I need or want because I am not important enough". When needs and desires are not met they become psychological hungers and eating becomes a way of feeding them as you will see in chapter 9.

Let's look again at Jacqui's story:

Jacqui was an overweight child. Her sister Marilyn was thin such that their mother worried a lot about her when they were young. Marilyn got a lot of attention. Jacqui did not feel that she got much attention, so began to think she was not important and from there decided she was not good enough to warrant attention. Later Marilyn grew into a very attractive teenager who looked and acted older than her years. She was always noticed and acknowledged by others. Jacqui often felt invisible and described being in a room full of people who always gathered around Marilyn, but never her. She would walk into the room and no one noticed. This heightened Jacqui's lack of self-esteem and self-worth and her sense of not being good enough. This feeling lasted for years into her adult life and she severely lacked confidence. Food became an important substitute, though Jacqui would sometimes overeat and sometimes withdraw from eating at all. At these starvation times, she felt frightened of eating, as if the food was her enemy. When she binged she would often dissociate from what she was doing and her body self. Thus, not realising how much she was eating, she did not stop until she felt sick. Jacqui had come to a number of conclusions which we can relate to her Young Parent.

Her negative Young Parent told her:

1. You are not important enough for attention. "Don't be important."
2. "You are obviously not good enough to be given attention."

   Jacqui ate, then found a reason to explain her sense of not being good enough which she lodged in her Young Parent:
3. "You are fat and fat is bad."

It was only when Jacqui could claim her sense of being important and good enough that she could lose weight. She needed to believe herself to be important and good enough in order to stop needing her body size to confirm her lack of worth. She had linked her size to the perceived lack of attention as a child, even though she had created this idea herself. "I am not good enough to be important. If I am fat, it makes sense that I won't be noticed. Being fat is bad. That gives them a good reason not to notice me".

We worked in therapy with Jacqui's belief that she was not important. She realised that she had not only made this conclusion from her experiences in the family dynamics but that she would also look for confirmation of this belief. So wherever she could deduce someone was ignoring her in favour of others she would reaffirm her lack of importance. What she then realised was that she would hang back in groups such that it was easy to miss her in favour of the more lively and confident members of the group. This was an intriguing way of endorsing her belief.

When Jacqui understood that she was carrying a "don't be important" injunction and then finding ways to reinforce it, she found release. She acknowledged this was a decision made when she was young and without the wherewithal to comprehend what was going on. She came to believe she was important and as a result, she didn't need to push her boundaries out and be big in the world. She concluded that she was not bad and therefore no longer needed to hide her "bad self" within body armour.

Check that you feel OK about answering the following questions. There is no obligation to do so.

Exercise 1

1. Have you ever felt unimportant? Thus could be at work, at home, or with certain people.
2. If yes, in what circumstances?

3. Do you think you may have made a conclusion of not being important from things that you experienced in childhood? If so, jot down a few ideas.

4. Now you are an adult and thinking rationally, will you accept that you are important as a human being and in your own right?
5. If "yes", that is wonderful. If "no", it is good you are recognising this. Now aim to think of four good and valid reasons why you are important. You can find them.

   a.
   b.
   c.
   d.

6. If you have not found four good reasons why you are important, imagine you are telling someone else, partner, family or friend that you feel you are not important and explain why. Jot down your thinking.

7. Would they agree with you?

---

8. If they wouldn't agree, what reasons would they give for not agreeing? Note them here:

9. If you are OK about how you have answered the questions write a few words to describe your feelings.

"*Don't be a child*". This means that the child would have been expected to take on responsibilities or actions beyond their age and would not have been allowed the freedom of childish play; they have to grow up too soon. This often results in needing to be "big", i.e. be a large size, to carry the burden of this injunction even into adulthood where life also feels burdensome. These people, as grown-ups, often take on extra responsibilities such that they feel weighed down. This provides the familiar feelings experienced in childhood and so the behaviour persists. As a consequence, they need to eat to be "big enough" to carry the extra weight of responsibility.

Exercise 2

If you have felt OK doing the previous exercise(s), continue with your self-exploration here.

1. When you look back to your childhood, do you feel you had to take on responsibilities beyond your age?
2. Do you, as an adult, often take on lots of extra things to please others?
3. Can you say "no" when asked to do things?
4. Do you have time for yourself?
5. Do you think that you are overburdened a lot of the time?
6. Do you think that you might unconsciously want to be big in order to shoulder responsibilities and burdens?

If you have answered yes to some of the above questions:

A. How do you think your larger body size is helpful to you?

B. Could you carry out your daily tasks without your larger size?

C. Can you enjoy fun, childlike things that take you away from adult responsibilities?

Childlike games and fun are important in releasing the Child from the injunction: "Don't be a Child."

D. What childlike things would you like to do? (E.g. paddling in a stream, jumping in puddles, swinging on swings etc.) Name three or more.

E. Give yourself permission to do the things you have listed. And then do them with someone else or by yourself as soon as you can. Write in this book or in your notebook what activities you have done and how you enjoyed them. Then do them again.

"Don't be close". When parents are unable to show love and affection their child may sense that they are not allowed to be close either. This can also mean that you cannot have physical contact and what better way to believe you can ensure this than by being a large size, pushing out the boundaries in an illusory attempt to keep people away? Even people who have partners can still believe this injunction. Making these decisions about ourselves is not a rational process and so we can always find a way of perpetuating them. The psychological hunger for closeness and all that that gives us in terms of validation and self-worth is so often fed with food.

We know that physical contact engenders a sense of well-being and acceptance and is very important in our development. Without it, we do not get the warmth and soothing or the recognition that we need. This unmet need becomes another psychological hunger and, again, the answer is to feed it with food.

Exercise 3

If you have felt OK doing the previous exercise(s), continue with your self-exploration here.

1. Were your parents or caregivers able to show their affection for each other?
2. Were your parents or caregivers able to demonstrate their love for you with hugs and kisses, loving words and actions?

If your answers are "yes" then it is unlikely you will have a "Don't be close" injunction. You can move on to the next relevant exercise.

If your answers are "no", it is worth thinking about whether you are carrying a "Don't be close" injunction, and whether this is contributing to your overeating and larger size.

Given that physical touch is important to our wellbeing:

A. Are you able to hug as much as you would like?
B. Are you able to receive hugs as much as you would like?
C. If not, who or what has indicated in your past that hugging isn't allowed?

D. How did they do that?

E. Do you feel at times that you keep your distance as if you think you might be rejected?
F. Do you think you might be unconsciously holding on to a larger size to keep others at a distance?

G. If so, what do you think about this?

H. If you feel you have been "given" a "Don't be close" injunction, do you think you might be eating to compensate for lack of closeness?
 I. What do you think about this?

J. What might you be able to do about it?

"Don't feel." Parent figures who shy away from showing feelings or repri-mand their child for crying or feeling fear, anger or even laughter, can inad-vertently give this command to their offspring. It can arise at two levels: one is not to express feelings that *are* felt and the other is simply not to feel at all. If a child is not allowed to show feelings, then it may result in emotions being held down by swallowing food. "Don't show emotion, just eat!" It might also be that the message is interpreted as "don't have feelings or physical sensations." Many people I have worked with have dissociated from body sensations and thereby are unable to distinguish true hunger pangs and to judge when they have eaten enough. Clients have reported eating until they are so full they feel bloated or sick. At this point, they can definitely feel something but it has taken this ex-treme action to find that sensation that says they have eaten enough. In fact, by this time, it is invariably too much.

Exercise 4

If you have felt OK doing the previous exercise(s), continue with your self-exploration here.

1. Did your parents or caregivers show their feelings?

2. Do you feel all your feelings such as sadness, anger, fear, happiness and all the related feelings like agitation,irritability etc. If not, which ones do you feel most.

3. Which ones do you feel least?

4. Do you think that there are times when you don't feel at all? Write down some examples that you have noticed.

5. Do you think you may be pushing down your feelings with food?

> **Think of some times that you might have done this. Jot down some examples.**
>
> 6. **What do you think will happen if you feel your feelings?**
>
> 7. **What do you think will happen if you show your feelings?**
>
> 8. **As an adult in your own right, what do you say about your answers to numbers 5, 6 and 7? Write down your thoughts:**
>
> 9. **Do you think there are times when you don't feel body sensations? Write down some examples you have noticed.**

In chapter 11 there are exercises enabling you to reconnect with your body self which will help you to recognise body sensations and the associated feelings.

"Don't be you." When a parent figure does not allow space for a young child to explore and experiment, and then imposes rules of how to be and indeed, how not to be, to the extent that the child feels confined, then that child may conclude that she or he cannot be his or herself. This injunction can also be carried if the child is continuously being compared to another sibling or friend who seems to be a "better" child. Perhaps the mother has an image of how a perfect child should be or perhaps the parent figures wanted a girl and had a boy, or wanted a boy and had a girl. This often shows in the children being given a name that could be either a boy or girl.

I have found that many overweight clients are carrying a "Don't be you" injunction. They are overweight when they don't want to be. They do not feel that being overweight is being themselves. It is not who they want to be. The adage "inside me there is a slim person waiting to come out" has some truth to it. The Body armour, i.e. fat, can be seen to hide and confine the Child that was restricted so acutely in childhood. A larger size might suggest power and protection for the Child within when she/he lacks the confidence to be his or herself.

Exercise 5

If you have felt OK doing the previous exercise(s), continue with your self-exploration here.

1. Were there times in your childhood when you felt put down and restricted in what you were able to do?

2. What happened?

3. Were there times when you thought it might be better to be someone else? If so, when?

4. Do you think that being the size you are is the real you? If not then:
5. Describe the real you that is waiting to come out:

6. Imagine welcoming that real you. What would you say?

7. Does it make sense to your adult, grown-up self, to be someone other than yourself?

8. In your grown-up voice, with your Adult ego-state engaged, will you say to your inner child: "You can be you. You can be the size you want to be. I will be there to help and guide you."

9. What was it like saying those words?

Alan's story is typical of the way this injunction might be received.

Alan's parents had rules as to what could be said and done inside and outside the house, as if there were secrets that no one should know about. There were strict rules about what could be discussed within the family and even more so when they had visitors. There was, however, a further complication in that the rules constantly changed. Alan desperately tried to be compliant in a somewhat chaotic world. Father was an angry man and had little relationship with his son. Mother controlled Alan's friendships, which sometimes resulted in Alan having few or even no friends at times in his childhood. Alan didn't know who he was but concluded that it wasn't OK to be himself. He has used his "body padding" to protect himself from the outside world to which he didn't feel he fit. Alan started to change his eating on realising that he could be his true self. He no longer needed to hide himself within body armour.

Alan said to me: "My 'don't be you' is only powerful if I accept it as the truth. I am the ultimate judge and I am the gatekeeper".

In summary, these types of messages in the Young Parent are very powerful. They have their origin in unconscious communication from parents and carers who clearly do not actually say "Don't be a child" or "Don't feel" etc. The infant, child or youngster makes these interpretations from what they experience or what they sense is implied. These self-constructed unconscious messages remain with us until we bring them into our awareness. When people have struggled with their weight and eating for a long time, I believe we need to attend to these "deeper" messages lodged in this Young Parent part of the Child ego-state.

It is important to know that injunctions can only persist if we give them the power to do so. Let us know look at how the Child in the Child functions.

Child in the Child

Once again, don't worry if you don't understand everything you read the first time. The questions will help you make sense of it in a way that is right for you.

The Child in the Child part of us also internalises our bodily experiences in response to the world around us. When I write about connecting with body sensations that tell us whether something is OK or not, or tell us when we are biologically hungry or whether we are experiencing discomfort in response to psychological hungers, it is this part of the Child ego-state that I have in mind.

Infant development and its relationship to overeating or maintaining a large body size

An infant initially experiences the world through body sensation. It is the means by which the world is understood and how the child starts to differentiate itself from its environment, i.e. "this is me here and I differ from that out there." In the first few months of life a child will also develop a sense of his or her body boundaries, differentiating between the inside and surface of the body. These are two very important stages in the infant's development. If these processes are inadequately delivered or interrupted, then the child may not have a clear sense of his or her body boundary and may not have the full sensation of knowing what is internal and what is external to the body.

This is significant in that people who need to be larger than they consciously want to be are using their body boundaries as protection, both pushing them out against the world or needing to "hide" within. (Anorexics pull in their boundaries to get away from the troublesome world.)

A further consequence of the interrupted development in establishing this vital sense of self is a disconnection from the body self and an inability, at times, to recognise and interpret body sensations. This includes determining whether we are hungry for food and knowing when we have eaten enough.

Because our body sensations occur in advance of cognitive recognition, it makes absolute sense that we can discover so much more about what is going on for us if we are attuned to our body selves. Our bodies can tell us stuff that the brain has not yet arrived at. Interpreting body sensation is what we did as babies and we need to reconnect with that skill as far as we can as adults. In this way, we learn to know when we are genuinely in need of food (biological hunger) and when we have eaten enough. We can then distinguish between the pangs of actual physical hunger and the sensations of what we call psychological hunger i.e. when we eat because there is something missing in our lives or when we are, for instance, anxious, sad, angry or fearful.

Somatic (body) memories are lodged in the Child in the Child which is why it is so helpful to listen to, and feel, our body sensations. They can tell us so much. Chapter 11 describes how you can reconnect with the body self and recognise body sensations.

The influence of early feeding patterns

Another area of particular interest for us is early feeding patterns. The body sensations related to feeding might be warmth, comfort, connection, caring, attunement, peace and a comforting fullness after being hungry. On the other hand, they might be feelings of being rushed, having colic, being overfed, not having enough, feeling a carer's stress and so forth. Using food to "resolve" unmet social and psychological needs and the idea of "comfort eating" may have its origins in these early bodily experiences. Once again, the memories of the body sensations of being fed are locked into the Child in the Child. Feeding is one of the most important factors of an infant's existence. When, as adults, things are not as good for us they might be, it is easy to understand that we would revert to feeding related to infancy as a possible resolution. As feeding and its associated sensations are at the centre of the early infant's existence, so eating becomes a focus in the adult when times get tough.

Here is a story that illustrates the power of early feeding.

Caroline was the youngest of five children. Her mother was asthmatic and during a bad coughing fit, she broke a rib. This brought on premature labour and Caroline was born. Her mother had to stay in hospital and so Caroline was given to the care of her paternal grandmother, Lexi, whilst the other children stayed home and were cared for by the maternal grandmother.

Lexi believed in chubby babies being healthy babies. Every time Caroline cried she would be fed again and again. If she was sick, Lexi would feed her more, thinking she needed to replace the food Caroline had expelled. She fed her as if she were a term baby instead of a six-week premature infant. After some weeks, Caroline was returned to her mother. She was dangerously overweight and had to be put on a diet.

As a teenager and adult Caroline's eating was erratic. Her pattern was to overeat, diet, undereat, lose weight, gain weight, diet. In a significant therapeutic moment whilst working with her Child ego-state Caroline was crying "Just hold me, don't feed me". This plea had never been in her awareness, even though her mother had told her what had happened in the first few months of her life. It was a revelation that changed Caroline's eating for life.

Exercise 6

1. **Write down a few points that you have been told about your early feeding patterns.**
2. **Were you called "a hungry baby"?**

3. **Were you overfed as a baby?**
4. **Was feeding easy for you?**
5. **Do you think feeding was a pleasurable experience for you?**
6. **Do you eat when stressed?**
7. **Do you sometimes feel agitated or impatient at mealtimes or other times when you believe the food is not there quickly enough? How does this feel?**

8. **If your answer in 7 is yes. Reflect for a moment on how old you feel at these times.**

9. **What do you notice about your answers?**

10. What patterns can you see emerging now in your adult life from thinking about your own early feeding?

11. What will you do when you find these associations in future?

Responses from the Child in the Child

Let us look further at the way the Child makes decisions about himself or herself.

If, in response to perceived parental messages, a child believes he or she is "bad" she/he may decide to be a large size to hide that "bad" self. A message such as "fat is bad" that might be from an actual parent, culture or internal Parent might further confirm the belief that "I am bad" - a belief that is held in the Child in the Child.

When a child concludes that a parent who is emotionally or physically absent doesn't love them, it is a short leap again to "I am unlovable" which we saw in Rowena's story. Lack of attention and feeling not good enough can lead to deep feelings of emptiness, both conscious and unconscious, which is the kind of sensation that relates to the Child in the Child. It can feel like a very profound body experience. That emptiness repeatedly drives people to eat in an attempt to fill the void and quell the feeling. One client said to me "I feel as though I need a hundred tons of food to fill that emptiness."

Everything that is lodged in these parts of our Child has essentially been in response to the people, and events that happen, around us. As we don't have the capacity to examine what our carers or more senior others are doing and saying, we make our own interpretations with our child-like thinking. These early unproven decisions continue to influence us out of awareness until we recognise and challenge them. As adults we have that capacity to really look at and understand what went on for us as children and above all, to recognise we are now our own people with the right to be and do things our own way. We can work out how we got to these erroneous conclusions about ourselves. We can, and need to, change those early beliefs and come to love, accept and value ourselves.

Not feeling good enough

Not feeling good enough is a recurrent belief in clients I have worked with over the years. Pauline was someone with great potential who had been limited by her sense of not being good enough. She had decided this in response to parents who, for significant periods of her life, were inattentive. Her parents divorced which Pauline took on as her fault because she wasn't good enough to keep them together. Pauline didn't apply for jobs that she wanted because of her lack of confidence due to her feelings of not being good enough. She constantly felt thwarted, agitated, and depressed. She tried to reduce her negative feelings by eating, but, like many others, the "satisfaction" gained from eating was short-lived and gave way to feelings of self-loathing. When Pauline shifted to believing she was (and is) good enough, things changed dramatically for her, including not feeling (psychologically) hungry and not reaching for extra food. Her Young Parent who told her she wasn't good enough was silenced at last and made way for the Child in her Child to become calm. She was able to make good new decisions. She is now in the job she has aspired to for years and above all, feels she deserves it. Her psychological need for food diminished almost automatically. She said "I have not felt hungry ... it is as though I am not hungry anymore. It's the strangest thing."

Of course, it is not actually strange. Once the main issue underlying the need to overeat has been resolved the extra food is no longer necessary. Nonetheless, people do seem surprised at the unplanned reduction in their need for food when they have resolved their psychological hungers.

Exercise 7

If you feel OK continue to answer these exploratory questions.

1. Are there times in your life that you have not felt "good enough". If so when?

2. What does "not good enough" really mean?

3. Thinking of the people's stories you have read so far, why do you think you might have this negative feeling?

4.   Think of five times when you *have felt* good enough and write them below.

5.   How is it that you *have felt* good enough at those times?

6.   Using your answer in question 5, how might you ensure you feel good enough more times than not?

In summary

It is important to recognise that our actual parents or caregivers have no idea of the infant conclusions we have made from their behaviours and sayings and would mostly be surprised, upset, and even shocked, at what we have deduced. It may well be that they have been inattentive, have expected their child to do things beyond their capabilities, have not induced feelings of self-worth, have not been or seemed close, etc., but they wouldn't know it. However, if we can discover how we got to believe negative things about ourselves, we can make new choices and decisions.

We give power to the injunctions until we recognise them, understand where they came from and know that we no longer need to follow them; we can then take back that power. So, understanding these underlying influences enables us to change the power in the Young Parent and the respective responses in the Child in the Child that keep the Adapted Child adapted.

Finally, here are some questions to bring your thoughts together.

Exercise 8

1.   What has impacted you most in what you have read in this chapter?

2.   Why do you think that is?

3.   Have you identified with any of the stories you have read? If so, which?

4.   How is your story similar?

5.   How is your story different?

6.   Name one or more things you have found helpful in answering the questions.

7.   Name one or more things you have found helpful in reading this chapter.

Note

1 You can read more about injunctions in "Injunctions, decisions and re-decisions" TAJ 6.1. 1976 by Bob and Mary Goulding.

Chapter 9

Psychological Hungers – Are you hungry for food or is it something else?

This chapter, like the last, reaches the more unconscious drives to overeat. Read through the explanation and then use the questions to discover some of the psychological hungers you are trying to satisfy with your eating or your size. At the end of the chapter, you will be asked what you think you can change and what new decisions you can make.

Remember your mantras, they will help you here:

> "I am OK", "I can think for myself", "I have choices and can make my own decisions" and "I am worth it".

Here are a few questions to lead you into this chapter:

- Do you sometimes feel agitated and in need of food immediately?
- Do you think that the extra food helps you get through the day or evening?
- Do you sometimes feel undervalued?
- Do you sometimes feel understimulated or bored?
- Do you sometimes feel invisible?
- Are there days when you don't see anyone to talk with?
- Are you happy with your work, whether at home or in the workplace?
- Do you want more cuddles, physical contact or sexual activity?

All these questions, if answered with a "yes", are likely triggers for your desire to overeat. They all relate to psychological and emotional hunger.

Physical Hunger is a result of a chemical reaction in the body that tells us we need to eat. It is normal to feel hunger pangs when the body needs energy. Generally in our culture, we have some form of regular meals or readily have access to food so, for many, strong hunger pangs are not often experienced.

If what we feel is pure physical hunger, and are not persuaded to eat by psychological hungers we are more likely to know when we have had enough to eat. We would stop eating at the point where our bodies and brains tell us

DOI: 10.4324/9781003240877-9

we have had enough. It clearly is not when we feel "stuffed" or un-comfortable, but that is sometimes the only point at which many of my clients do know they have had enough. Many of us eat more than we need from time to time, e.g. when out for a meal or having friends for dinner, or on some special occasion. Social eating is part of our culture. We make choices to celebrate, entertain and treat ourselves to a meal out, etc. so we need to make decisions to do this from our Adult selves. That way, we do not have to listen to internal voices in our heads telling us we shouldn't be doing this. If we make the decision from our Adult thinking selves, there is less opportunity for the Child to rebel and overindulge.

When we constantly eat more than we need physically, we are almost certainly responding to one or more psychological hungers or needs. Of course, there is no resolution in overeating, it solves nothing and can actually cause more distress. If you do feel "better" for eating, it is usually short-lived and then, in many cases, there is a negative feeling that follows for having eaten so much. Often these feelings are of sadness or anger, disappointment, or even disgust.

Psychological hunger can often be mistaken for physical hunger. Psychological hunger is never physical hunger even though it sometimes feels as though there is a physical need for food. When there is an attempt to satisfy psychological hunger with food, we eat more than we need and the weight goes on.

We need to learn to distinguish between these two sets of hunger so that we can truly know if we need food or something else. It is the psychological hunger that drives us to eat more than we need and not physical hunger.

Though we use the word "hunger", it might be helpful to think of it as "need". Use whichever word helps you most. Psychological needs are about something that is disturbing, worrying, missing or unresolved and never about the need for food.

The founder of TA (Transactional Analysis) Eric Berne described three main types of psychological hunger, they are:

1 Hunger or need for stimulus or, more helpfully, "stimulation"
2 Hunger or need for Structure in our lives
3 Hunger or need for Recognition i.e. To be loved, acknowledged and recognised or noticed

People may respond differently to each of these hungers, seeking out satisfaction through other behaviours but we are specifically considering how they play a part in overeating. When you start to see that you are not always genuinely in need of food, you will have the choice to consider what it is that you really need, and when you know what that is, you can make changes.

As we have discussed, the action of reaching for extra food at these times comes from the **Child** within us (Child ego-state). When we start to investigate what is happening at these times, we are using our **Adult** selves

(Adult ego-state). As you now know, it is our Adult selves that can work out what to do differently. At the same time, we need to listen to, and be compassionate with, our Inner Child.

Let's look at each of these hungers in more detail. After each one there are questions for you to answer that will extend your understanding.

Stimulus Hunger or need for stimulation

From birth we thrive, grow and learn about the world through stimulation. We use our senses: sight, hearing, smell, touch, and taste. When an infant has had enough stimulation s/he will fall asleep. Experiments have shown that when an infant does not have enough stimuli, s/he will not thrive in the way other children who have that stimulation do. As adults, we continue to need that stimulation, albeit, clearly in more grown-up ways.

The words that might come to mind immediately, perhaps, are monotony and boredom. It may be that there is not enough to do or to occupy the mind or the tasks in hand are boring and repetitive. This under-stimulation can cause feelings such as tiredness, agitation, hopelessness and depression and all these can force us to try to find solace in food.

I have often found that people whose work or daily lives are not offering enough stimulation turn to food as if it can provide some significant stimulus. Whilst choosing and eating the food, enjoying the flavours and textures, it can feel as though something positive is happening but that feeling is, of course, short-lived. It does not resolve the problem. Food has given a sense of temporary relief but it has changed nothing. It certainly has not satisfied the need for something more stimulating in our lives. It tends to result in waiting impatiently for the next snack or not waiting at all.

Questions for you:

1. **Are you fulfilled in your work or your day, whether at home or in your workplace?**

2. **Can you identify what you feel immediately before reaching for food? If so, write what you have discovered here. If not, make it an aim to discover what it is you feel.**

3. Do you reach for food when you feel bored, frustrated, dissatisfied or unstimulated?

4. If yes, what foods do you reach for most?

5. What is significant about these foods?

6. Can you think about how you could make life more interesting whether in work or outside of it so that you feel more fulfilled? I encourage you to seek at least one thing. The answer is within you. A few small things could really make a difference.

This brings us to the next psychological need.

Structure hunger or need for some level of purposeful activity

This need relates well to the first one. Structure is provided by having an aim in the day, a meeting with someone, whether social or work-related; a job to go to; something to plan for in the future; maybe someone to look after. We need meaningfulness in our lives and need to feel we have a purpose. The level of this need will differ from person to person, but it is always there in some form.

Monica, one of my clients, was at home alone during the day and part of the evening. Her two children had left home and her husband worked long hours, often even bringing work home. She had not worked since having her children and never felt she had time for hobbies whilst bringing up the boys and latterly caring for her aged mother who had moved to a nursing home. Now, however, she felt as though she had no purpose in life. The days were long and lonely and she had no structure to her day. She saw how she was putting that structure into her day by eating. She would eat breakfast, lunch and tea by herself and dinner with her husband when he eventually came home. She snacked regularly during the day such that snack times became a ritual and then she picked more food between snack times for something to do. When her husband was working after dinner, she would feel lonely and compensate with more snacks. She would often eat bags of crisps or chocolate mindlessly in front of the television, becoming rather surprised when they had all gone. She was not aware of how much she was eating. The behaviour had become automatic.

Monica was not only feeding the emptiness she felt, but she was also structuring her day by eating. She recognised that on days when she did some specific household chores she would eat less. When she went out to meet a friend, she would eat less during the day. When she added more structure to her days by having certain times and days to do certain jobs and arranging to go out of the house more often to shop or meet friends, she reported feeling better and eating less. She eventually took a part-time job and started a course in bookkeeping and her eating became much less of an issue. She lost a very significant amount of weight. She regained her self-esteem which further helped her to think about what and when she ate extra food. She now believed she was worth it.

In the process of her therapy, we had examined what thoughts and feelings she experienced just before the point of reaching for food. We began to understand that lack of structure in her life had seriously dented her feelings of self-worth and confidence. This in turn had caused her to do less and less, neglect herself and rapidly gain weight. She gradually added more non-food structure to her day as she progressively valued herself and by doing so, her confidence grew to the point where she was able to seek and gain that part-time post and enrol on the course.

Questions for you:

1. **Write down ways that you recognise you structure your day.**

2. **Does this provide enough structure for you?**

3. **Do you provide structure by eating? If so write down when, what and how you eat.**

4. What do you notice about what you have written in question 3 regarding what you eat, when you eat and how you eat?

5. Now think about why you eat at these times. Write a few notes.

6. What might you do instead of eating? What might you put in place so that you are not drawn to eating in this way?

Monica's changes were not only about practical differences but about self-worth and self-esteem and this was enhanced by the fact that she was being **recognised**. This brings us to a third hunger: that of recognition.

Recognition hunger. Or the need for recognition. Known in TA as "strokes"

When I referred previously to the fact that infants need stimulation in order to thrive, what they also need is touch, stroking, holding and mirroring of their own expressions by their parents or carers. In research carried out some years ago, it was observed that babies in children's homes who did not get this physical contact and mirroring did not thrive as well as others. We continue to need this sort of recognition as adults. However, we clearly cannot have the close nurturing style of infancy. So we have different ways of getting this need fulfilled. We need people to respond to us and to acknowledge us. We need appropriate touch and physical contact. As adults, we can't be cuddled and held in the same way as infants nor have the intensity of attention that an infant needs, so we substitute this physical contact for other ways of knowing we are here and belong to something outside of ourselves. We need **recognition.**

Types of recognition range from a nod of acknowledgement by someone in the street, a "how are you?" from the check-out lady at the supermarket, a smile from people around us, to praise and compliments, partnerships, marriage, love, intimacy and sexual activity. You will see that the level of intimacy grows from the "nod" to the full-blown relationship. In TA we call these "strokes" of recognition. All such strokes of recognition are important for our well-being and sense of self.

If we are stroke-deprived we are unfulfilled, as we saw in Monica's story. We can feel worthless and lacking in confidence, depressed and alone in the world. Monica was alone a lot of the day; her husband arrived home late and often had to work after dinner. There were few people around her to acknowledge her. Again, food is so frequently used to try to get that feeling of being stroked or to hold down the sadness and feed the emptiness. We can really underestimate the importance of social and physical contact and it is one of the major areas for investigation when looking at overeating and binging patterns. When there is interaction at whatever level, you are being stroked. If we are low in self-esteem and confidence, not only are we more likely to stay away from others, we are also unlikely to receive these strokes as recognition of ourselves. We deny strokes that are given to us by saying such things as "she didn't mean it!", or "he was only being polite", "they didn't really want to talk to me". This is called "discounting" the strokes we could otherwise internalise.

Questions for you:

Looking back on the last few days:

1. **When and where did you receive a stroke such as a nod, a smile, a "how are you today", or "what weather we are having!" or anything in this line? They are all strokes.**

   If you cannot recall any, make a point of looking out for these sorts of strokes tomorrow.

2. **Have you received any compliments or praise recently? If so list them.**

If you don't think you have received any praise or compliments, or don't remember any, don't worry, this is just a starting point to get to know what your stroke "picture" is. You will learn how to increase your pot of strokes. But be sure to listen and watch out for these important strokes, however small.

Recognising how you use strokes is central to understanding the deeper issues that relate to your need for that extra food and bigger size.

It is important for our well-being to build up a "stroke pot"; to be aware of when and where we are stroked and to value it. The more strokes we collect the better we feel about ourselves. An empty stroke pot leads to filling the pot with food!

Here are some ways to recognise when you refuse strokes and positive ways of filling your stroke pot.

a   **It is very easy for someone with low self-esteem to ignore and reject positive strokes.**

For example, someone compliments you on your hair, your jumper, your piece of work or says she/he likes your attitude to something or likes, or loves you. If you are low in self-worth, you will almost certainly reject these strokes. You may say in response to someone liking your jumper "oh, I've had it ages." Or when someone says you have done a good piece of work, you may say to yourself or out loud to that person: "Anyone could have done that". You may say to yourself, "they are just being kind, they don't mean it" and you may say to yourself "I am not worth it". All these are examples of ways in which we might discount the nice things said to us. Each time we do this, we miss the opportunity to "swallow" the stroke, i.e. really let it in and know its value and thereby our own value. Instead, we swallow food!

Sometimes if we are feeling low about ourselves, we can't even hear strokes but are very quick to dismiss the ones we do see and hear. You just need to keep listening and watching. If someone gives you a stroke, your task is to listen and accept it! You can teach yourself to feel as though you are swallowing that positive stroke, so that you really do let it in. Imagine swallowing down a positive stroke; imagine that stroke passing down from your mouth to your throat, feel it go to your chest and down into your tummy. Feel its warmth.

Questions for you:

1   **Think about the last few days and write down how you have refused strokes, wherever they have come from.**

2   **Have you told yourself that you are not worthy of praise, or have you outwardly denied or belittled something to someone giving you praise? Jot down how you have done this.**

3.   Have you told yourself they are not worthy to give you a compliment?

Over the next few days, listen for strokes and see if you are tempted to discount them either in your head or verbally to the other person. We do it far more often than we realise. Write them at the back of this book or in your own book. And from now on, try to let them in.

b.   **You can also give yourself strokes**. We are often uneasy about this one. Parental words like "Don't blow your own trumpet" prevent us from praising ourselves. You yourself can recognise a good piece of work that you have done and be proud of it. You can see that your hair looks nice and you can acknowledge this for yourself. In fact, it is very important to compliment yourself in as many ways as possible. Receiving strokes from others, if you allow them in, can feel good and you need them, but knowing for yourself how "good" and "worthwhile" you are, in any circumstances, provides a very solid base for your sense of OKness which, in itself, will help you to move to a position where you do not need extra food.

It can feel really confirming when you are willing to recognise and acknowledge what you do well, what you like about yourself and who you are. Try it! Of course, the ultimate would be that you can tell someone else how good you are at something, how you are pleased with a purchase, or how nice you have been to someone. But if that seems a bridge too far, why not tell yourself, out loud if possible but, otherwise, in your head. When you allow yourself to do this it feels very strengthening. Why would you not recognise your own achievement or thing well done or how lovely you are? It is fine to know it.

Questions for you:

1.   In the last few days have you praised or complimented yourself?
2.   If you have answered yes, write down when and how.

3.   If you have answered "no" write down why not. Your answer must not be that there is nothing to praise because that is not the truth for anyone.

4. **Write down three things you like about yourself.**

c. **We can ask for strokes.** I suspect you are thinking that you couldn't possibly ask someone for a stroke. But maybe you already do? Do you ever say, for instance, "did you like that meal I cooked ?" or "do you like these shoes I got in the sale? "Do you like what I've done?" Well, you are asking for strokes! You can build up your confidence in asking. Don't be put off by any disappointing replies, someone has responded and thought about what you are asking. They have recognised you! Usually, there will be a positive response, and your next step is to hear and accept that positive stroke.

Questions for you:

1. **Have you ever asked for a stroke?**

2. **If the answer is "yes" note down when and what it was you asked for. (Well done you!)**

3. **If the answer is "no", write down why not.**

4. **Will you promise yourself you will ask for a stroke as soon as you can? What might you ask?**

d. **You can give strokes to others**. It is amazing how often we withhold strokes from others. Sometimes it feels embarrassing to give someone a nice compliment or to praise them. Often this is accompanied by a belief that they will think "who is he or she to tell me my work is good or I look nice?" We will walk along the street or be next to someone in a supermarket or shop and never think of smiling or nodding, or making a comment about the fruit or the helpful assistant. It is true that more often than not, you will get a positive response from the other person. This adds to your positive stroke pot. It can make you feel good about yourself. Especially if you give quite a few strokes in a day. Try it!

It is, nevertheless, also true that people who suffer with their weight are often the ones that give the most to others in terms of helping and caring. Their positive Nurturing Parent is often active towards others but missing towards themselves. So it might be that you give lots of strokes to others, whether in the form of help, caring or verbal praise, and few, if any, to yourself.

Questions for you:

In the last few days how often have you:

1. Given a stroke to someone you didn't know? Note down when and what you said or did.

2. Done something for someone else? Note down when and what you did.

3. Said something nice to someone you know well? Note down when and what you said.

4. What did you feel when you did this?

5. What do you think they felt?

6. What strokes might you give tomorrow and who to?

e. **Contact Hunger. Physical contact such as hugs, holding hands, sitting closely alongside someone, touching and sexual activity are very valuable strokes for everyone.** This is a more intimate level of recognition. We never lose that physical need that we had as infants. I have found that many of my clients, whether men or women, who have presented with issues of overeating and being overweight have been deprived of warm and loving physical contact from early in their lives and have substituted food for this comfort. Hence their larger size has been a long-term problem. In my experience, many people struggling with being overweight don't feel they should have physical closeness and hugs or feel too big to be hugged. Some even feel that it would be embarrassing to be cuddled because the person giving the hug would feel their fat, and even experience disgust. I always find this very sad. But there is not one of my clients who has felt this way who has not changed their belief and asked for hugs from their family and partners once they give themselves permission to do so, through exploration and understanding.

Questions for you:

1. Do you feel you get enough physical contact or would you like more?

2. Can you ask for a touch or a hug from a partner, family or friend? If yes, well done you! Note down who.

3. If no, then write down why not.

4. Does your answer to 3 make sense to you when you use your Adult to think about it?

5. Will you make it your aim to ask for physical contact of some kind over the next few days?

6.   **Who will you ask?**

7.   **How will you ask?**

So often I have found that when a client desperately wants the closeness of holding and hugs but withdraws from them and doesn't ask for them, she/he has reached for food to try to quell the need. If I put what people say about this into a diagram it looks like this (Figure 9.1).

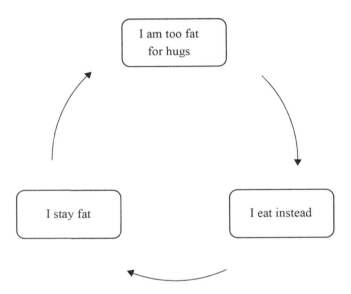

Figure 9.1 Cyclical thoughts regarding weight and hugs.

I have worked with many clients who fear close contact. Once they have worked through the necessary psychological issues they have been able to hug, be held and to ask for this from their partner, family members or friends. They have invariably found a positive response from those they asked. However, some people really do not like physical contact, whether because of injunctions, parental modelling, the absence of physical stroking as an infant or something else. If this is you, you must decide whether you want to explore this further or stay with the status quo. Whatever is right for you.

Sexual hunger

Sexual activity is also a form of stroking at a very intimate level. Sexual activity from teenage to old age is a natural part of relationships and a very normal drive. Sexual activity in women who are overweight/obese is often irregular, rarely entered into or absent altogether. This is not, in my experience, as prevalent in men. This has been reported as being because of the negative feelings about body size, shape and the texture of the fat around the body and is the same for males and females. Just as my clients have not asked for cuddles because they have felt that a partner would be disgusted with their bodies, they will avoid sexual activity for the same reasons. Some say they are unattractive even if their partners want a sexual relationship with them. The story is that: "I am fat" therefore I am unattractive, therefore no one would want sex with me, not even my partner." or "I am too ashamed of my body to have sex". Frequently it has been the lack of sexual activity that has driven the sufferer to eat instead. Again, this forms a vicious circle (Figure 9.2): relationship between sexual activity and body size

I can't have sex ◄─────────────► I eat to compensate and grow bigger

Figure 9.2 Relationship between sexual activity and body size.

Sexual activity is recognised as good for emotional and physical health and well-being. It is an important part of life. It produces a deeper level of bonding with a partner which in turn provides some of those much needed positive strokes.

Unless there is a real organic or physical reason why you cannot have a sexual relationship, then you can be sexual. You can enjoy sex, whatever your size or shape. A satisfying sexual relationship does not necessarily mean penetrative sex. You can enjoy sexual play together, or by yourself. You can reach a climax with great satisfaction if you allow yourself to do so. Talk with your partner about it. It is interesting that even in days of sexual liberation , talking about sex is still considered to be embarrassing. But you can do it! If you have a partner who seems to avoid the topic, you can be the grown-up with your Adult in charge and argue the case for a discussion about what affects you both. Or you could seek out a sex counsellor to aid the discussion. You do not, of course, need a partner for sexual gratification. Self-stimulation can be enjoyable and satisfying. It is not taboo!

Questions for you:

1.   Do you think that you have enough sexual contact?
2.   If not, note down why you think that is.

3.   Have you talked to your partner about your sexual relationship?
4.   If not, why not?

5.   Do you practice self-stimulation?
6.   If not, why not?

7.   Can you see how you might be using food to try to fill the gap left by some level of sexual disappointment? Note down a few thoughts.

All these needs or hungers, if misunderstood, ignored and not responded to, will lead to an attempt to meet them with food. The impulse to eat comes from an emotional place and from the sensation of sadness, anger or fear in response to these needs. As previousy noted, these sensations can be misinterpreted as biological hunger and a need for food. Psychological hunger can be experienced as physical hunger which gives a false indication that food is needed. It is also fact that the emptiness caused by the lack of strokes can lead to overeating food in an effort to fill that emptiness. This leads to low self-esteem, which triggers over-eating and becomes a cyclical experience. This is illustrated in the diagram below (Figure 9.3): relationship between strokes and weight gain.

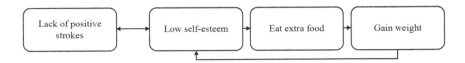

Figure 9.3 Relationship between strokes and weight gain.

You now know, if you feel the urge to eat and think you are biologically hungry when you have not long eaten, it is unlikely to be food you need. Check out your stroke picture as described above. Imagine you have a large pot ready to receive strokes. This pot needs to be pretty full. If it is low in strokes, or even empty, you will suffer from a lack of self-worth and self-esteem and we know that this is one of the major issues for those experiencing problems with weight- gain and overeating. So think about collecting your strokes. Strokes that you receive, give to others, give to yourself and ask for, all go into your stroke pot. Keep track of them in the back of this book (Figure 9.4).

Lots of positive strokes

Feel good about yourself - no need to eat food to compensate for lack of self-esteem

Figure 9.4 Stroke pot.

Chapter 10

What your body size might mean to you

As I have mentioned before, sometimes the problem with one's size is not always just about eating that extra food. Sometimes it is the weight and size itself that is important. This may sound strange when you want to lose weight but it is worth checking this out for yourself. In this chapter, we look specifically at this issue.

Many of my clients have come to realise that they have unconsciously needed the larger size to feel safe in the world. Some large men and women believe they are unattractive and therefore they don't have to deal with advances from potential partners of any gender or identification or, at a deeper level, some men and women unconsciously feel that they can keep the world at bay by pushing out their own body boundaries thus maintaining some sense of distance from others. Some need to be big to carry the burdens of their life on their shoulders. Some have had to fulfil tasks beyond their years in their childhood and so have had to be big enough to cope. For some, it is about feeling potent or strong. And for some there is a history of sexual abuse, abuse of their sexuality or physical abuse which has meant they need to stay large, protected by their fat as if it is armour around the body. As we saw in Chapter 8, some injunctions unconsciously "received" into the Child can lead to needing to be big in the world.

These are just a few of the reasons why people may unconsciously want to maintain a large body size.

If you have tried to lose weight on numerous occasions and have either lost nothing or lost and then regained the weight, often putting even more back on each time, it is worth looking at whether you unconsciously want to be that bigger size. That is not to say that the extra food is not also the issue, there are often multiple layers to our need for food. But if you do have this psychological need to be big in the world it is worth finding that out, so that you can work on bringing that need into consciousness. If you find that you have needed a large body to feel safe in the world, and then work through the underlying issues, it follows that you will no longer need extra food.

If you do think that you are eating more because you need to hold on to your heavier weight it is perfectly possible to resolve this problem, as we saw

DOI: 10.4324/9781003240877-10

with Rowena. If, however, you have experienced sexual abuse or similar trauma, then I do suggest you see a therapist or counsellor. Working through this book can only take you so far, especially if you have never talked to anyone about your history. If you find that you feel afraid of losing weight then you need to decide whether you need face to face help from a therapist or counsellor. You are in charge of yourself and can make your own decisions. Keep yourself safe in ways you learnt in chapter 1.

There are two easy and straightforward exercises that will help you determine whether you need your larger body size. These are also recorded on my website "My food space".

Exercise I

Sit somewhere comfortable and warm.

When you have read and understood the exercise that follows, close your eyes, if that feels OK, or keep them open and focus on one spot on a wall.

Exercise: Visualize yourself as the size you think you want to be. This must be a size that is achievable and not a skinny prince or princess!

Keeping your eyes closed or focussed, feel what goes on in your body, especially around your abdomen and chest. Notice the messages that go through your head. Be intrigued by what you feel. Give yourself time to be in touch with your body sensations and then open your eyes.

Now make a note of what you experienced.

1. Write down your physical sensations:

2. Write down the messages that went through your head.

3. Now reflect on your physical sensations and messages. What do they mean to you? Did you feel OK as you envisaged yourself slimmer? Did you feel any anxiety?

> **4. Do you think you might be staying a large size for some psychological reason? Write down your thoughts.**

If you have experienced any sensations of fear or discomfort at being thinner, then it might be you are hanging on to your weight in order to feel protected in the world. Be aware of this and you decide if want to find a practitioner to help you work it through. If you have felt no uncomfortable sensations in your tummy , chest or any other area of your body, then it is likely it is not the large size that you need. Your overeating will be for other reasons considered in this book.

If you have felt some stirring in your body during the exercise, ask yourself these questions:

1. **What am I afraid of?**

2. **Does my weight really protect me?**

3. **If I believe my weight protects me, how does it do that?**

4. **Why am I using my weight rather than figuring out what I need with my Adult self?**

5. **If I lose weight, what do I believe will happen?**

6. **As my grown-up self, how will I prevent that from happening?**

If you do feel you are afraid to lose weight then I do advise you to talk to a counsellor, therapist or another practitioner so you can work through that fear. If you feel OK, continue exploring further in this chapter.

Exercise 2

After reading the exercise, prepare yourself as you did with the first exercise, closing your eyes or focussing on the spot on the wall.

Exercise: you now need to see yourself as you are now. Do this for a minute and be in touch with the sensations you feel and the words that might be going on in your head. Then open your eyes and look at the questions that follow.

Questions:

1.   What sensations were you aware of in your body?

2.   What thoughts and words went through your head?

3   Think about what you have written and write down your observations.

4.   Are you clear that you want to lose weight?

Explanation

If you reflect on these exercises and the responses you have written, you will know whether you have some unconscious need to stay big or whether that is not an issue for you.

I believe that our body sensations are manifested by the Child within. If you have felt some anxiety or fear at being thinner, then it is your Child that is fearful. We know that the Child within us holds childhood sensations, and encounters and childhood memories. Sometimes these can be obscure and sometimes easily recalled.

So, things you might want to determine initially are:

"What is it that makes my Child feel fearful or anxious"? and

"What happened when I was a child or teenager that has made me think I need a large body size?"

Write your thoughts here:

"Do I feel able to explore this further, using this book?"

"Do I think I can be OK without my body armour?"

If your answer to the final question is "yes", you can continue to work on your weight loss journey. If your answer is "no", you might want to continue with the help of a therapist. You can, of course, continue to read the chapters and work with the parts that are right for you.

There follows another exercise using imagery that you might find helpful. You need to prepare yourself again in the same way as you did for the other exercises after you have read what to do next. So, you will be sitting comfortably and closing your eyes or focussing on the wall, as before. You might have someone to read the exercise to you if this feels OK. Or you can memorise it, or you may like to record it for yourself and then listen to your recording. You could also listen to it on my website:www.myfoodspace.-co.uk It is your choice.

Exercise 3   This is about creating a safe space for yourself

Imagine yourself walking to somewhere you feel safe. It might be somewhere you really do feel totally relaxed and safe in or you can imagine and create your own image. Enter your safe space. Look around your space and notice what you see around you. Take time to do this. Settle yourself, standing, sitting or lying within this space, choosing somewhere comfortable and warm and peaceful. Feel that peacefulness. Relax in your safe space. This is somewhere where no one else can enter unless you want them in there with you. You can invite anyone you want and deny access to anyone you don't want. This is your space. You may have windows to see out or you may have no windows, it is your choice. With your own powers, you can see if anyone is coming but until you allow them, they cannot see you or your own space.

You are perfectly safe. You can come here whenever you want and it takes only a second to get here. No one can see you or hear you unless you want them to. Enjoy being in your safe space. Feel soothed and calm. Feel peaceful in your space.

When you are ready, think again about losing the weight that you want to lose. Think about being safe with that choice. If fears arise, just project them onto the wall of your safe space, where you can watch them float by and disappear. You have the power to change them, to reduce their powers and to send them out of your space. They have no business here.

In your safe space, you may be able to take your body armour off. Imagine taking that onesie of fat off and putting it aside for now. Be aware of how that feels. You can put it on again whenever you need to, but for now, try and keep it off while you see what is going on for you. You are still in your safe space and this is just about you and for you. Keep in touch with how it is feeling to have taken off your extra weight.

When you are ready, put that armour back on. Just note how that feels for you.

Stay in your safe space as long as you like and then imagine yourself leaving it, securing it and coming back into the here and now.

Notice things around you in the room you are in. Identify things in the room where you are now. This can be out loud or to yourself. e.g. That is a chair; that is the light; this is the carpet or floor etc. This will ground you back in the present.

Questions:

(Answer each of them in your head first whilst you are still in touch with your safe space. Then note down your thoughts to keep for your reference.)

1. What was that like for you?

2. Did you feel your own sense of power?

3. Recall what your space was like and jot down a few words to describe it.

4. How did you feel in there?

5. Did you have any fears? And if so, what did you do with them?

6. How did you feel after throwing out your projected fears?

7. Write your notes about that experience and/or you may wish to draw your safe space. If there is not enough room, use the pages at the back of the book.

I hope you have felt something of your own potency in doing the safe space exercise. It is an exercise that appeals directly to your Child ego-state which is why it can be so effective. Remember, you can return to that space whenever you want. You can be there in a heartbeat. When you "project" your fears or anxieties onto the wall you will feel more able to see them as they are and feel your own power to deal with them. This includes knowing that it is OK for you to lose weight; you will still be safe in the world. Nothing is insurmountable. Everything has a solution.

What we certainly know is that the idea of a large body size keeping you safe in the world is an illusion. You are the one that has the power to keep yourself safe. You have potency which you can develop and you have an Adult self that can make decisions and choose who you want to be, what you want to do and where, how and when you want to do it.

Repeat the safe space exercise as often as you can. It will nourish you. You might change it, maybe add to it; you might even have more than one. It is an especially useful technique to calm your inner Child, whenever she/he feels scared, anxious, challenged or generally uneasy.

Chapter 11

Reconnecting with your body self

As I have explained before, we lose some of the ability to interpret body sensations as we grow. From birth, a baby knows when it is hungry and when it has had enough milk. It will cry when hungry and drop the nipple or teat and rest or sleep when it has had enough. It knows its needs through body sensations.

As those of us in a plentiful society go through life we start to eat according to "rules" and schedules rather than listening to our own bodies. Gradually, of course, our bodies become accustomed to the daily landmarks of breakfast, lunch and dinner (or some similar routine.) We get to have a necessary routine around eating times because a worker cannot just go off and have lunch whenever she/he feels like it and school children can't eat willy-nilly throughout the day. A good deal of social life revolves around eating at the generally recognised mealtimes. In this way, we move away from our natural sensations of hunger and replete-ness.

Add to this the need to eat for psychological reasons and the issue becomes even more complex. We lose the connection with the body self that is accurate in indicating true hunger pangs. In fact, it might be that we lose connection with the body self, full stop. This is a type of dissociation which is often apparent with my overweight clients. Some feel little sensation at all; others do not even recognise discomfort or pain or cold in parts of their body. Some dissociate by never looking at their bodies in the mirror and some do not even look at their faces.

There is a strong and indivisible link between body and mind. As infants, we develop a body self alongside a psychological self. They are not separate entities but each affects the other in significant ways. Your psychological self affects your eating and body size and your body size affects your sense of self. Your body gives you many messages through different sensations and, if allowed, will give you important information before your thinking head. Therefore, it is crucial in your journey to reconnect to your body self and feel the sensations and ultimately to accurately interpret them.

I suggest four tasks for you to use to reconnect with your body. You could do these by yourself or with someone you feel close to and someone you know will understand. If with someone else, you might ask them to read the

DOI: 10.4324/9781003240877-11

task out and then you can do the same for them. Maybe you could record the tasks and then listen to your recording. Or perhaps you can just memorise the stages. Or you might want to listen to them on my website: www.myfoodspace.co.uk. If you have an image of the outline of a body in your mind, it is easy to work from head to toes through that image.

The tasks involve a simple meditative process. If you are doing this by yourself, you will, of course, need to read it first. The best way to do this exercise is to sit in a chair or lie on the bed (make sure you stay awake).

The first task is to concentrate on each part of your body and discover what you are feeling.

Concentrate well on your stomach and abdomen as these are the areas that are particularly good at telling you when something doesn't feel right.

Exercise 1

Take a few slow deep breaths; breathe in as much air as you can, puff the air out slowly and deliberately through your lips. Do this two or three times and as you breathe out imagine your body sinking into the chair or bed and allow your muscles to let go. Slowly and deliberately, think about each part of your body starting with the head, then your neck, your shoulders and arms, your hands, your back and your chest, your tummy, then the legs, thighs, calves and finally feet and toes. Make sure they are as relaxed as possible.

Now breathe normally and read what to do next, then close your eyes or focus on a spot on the wall.

Very slowly and with care, work down through your body again; be in touch with sensations you feel in the different areas. Is your face relaxed or can you feel that your jaw is tight? Are you biting on your teeth? Are you frowning? Are your head and neck areas tense?

What are you sensing around those areas?

Are your shoulders hunched? Do those muscles feel tight?

Is your back rested or do you feel some discomfort, tension or pressure?

What about your chest? Do you feel some sensation there? Linger on this area for a while. It can tell you so much. Are you breathing normally or are you taking shorter breaths or holding your breath?

Are your arms relaxed or tensed? Are your hands floppy or clenched into fists or pushing down?

What is happening around and in your tummy now? Does it feel relaxed? Is it tight? Are you holding it tightly? Do you have feelings like butterflies? What else is happening?

What is happening in your legs? Your thighs and calves? Are they relaxed or pushed into the chair or bed?

Concentrate on your feet? Are they relaxed or pushed into the floor or towards the bed? Are your toes slightly curled?

After resting for a moment or two, reflect on what you experienced and what sensations you felt in your body. Jot down a few words about what you noticed.

Exercise 2   Add tension and release as you visit each part of your body.

Read through the exercise if you are doing this by yourself. (You can ask someone to slowly read it to you, or you can find it on my website.)

When I say "let go" it means to let your muscles relax. You can do this as a short sudden letting go or a gradual release.

As in Exercise 1, take a few good deep breaths and after you breathe in as much air as you can, puff the air out slowly and deliberately through your lips. Do this two or three times and as you breathe out imagine your body sinking into the chair or bed and allow your muscles to let go. Very slowly check your head and neck, your eyes, nose and mouth, your shoulders and arms, your back and your chest, your tummy, then the legs, thighs, calves and finally feet and hands. In other words, work your way down your body from head to toes, checking each part and each limb on the way. Make sure they are as relaxed as possible.

Now breathe normally. Read through what to do next and then close your eyes or focus on a spot on the wall.

Slowly with care, go through your body again; be in touch with sensations you feel in the different areas.

Your face: Is your face relaxed or can you feel that your jaw is tight? Are you biting on your teeth? Are you frowning? Are your head and neck areas tense? What are you sensing around those areas? Now, squeeze these areas tighter and then let go.

Now your shoulders: Are your shoulders hunched? Do your muscles feel tight? What do you feel? Now tense your shoulders more, hold, and then let go.

Your back: Is your back rested or do you feel some discomfort? Move around a little, tighten your back muscles then allow your back to sink into the bed or the back of the chair and let go.

What about your chest? Do you feel some sensation there? Linger on this area for a while. It can tell you so much. Are you breathing normally or are you taking shorter breaths? Take a deeper breath, tighten, hold and then let go.

Think about your arms and hands. Tense your arms really tightly move them a little and then just let go. Now squeeze your hands into fists, really tight and then let go.

Pull your tummy in tight, really hold it and then let go.

Tense your thighs, hold and let go.

Pull your toes up towards your legs and feel the tightness in your calves, hold it and then let go.

Now push your feet away from you or into the floor. Hold that tension and then let go.

Finally, tighten every part of your body, really squeezing tight and then let go.

Relax for as long as you are able.

Now reflect on what that was like for you. Note down where you felt particular tension, or where you found it difficult to let go.

Make a note of these tense areas.

Keep aware of these areas as you go about your day and repeat the tensing and releasing.

Exercise 3   Concentrating on your body sensations externally

In this exercise you just need to sit in a comfortable chair and again, you will close your eyes or keep your gaze on a blank spot on the wall. You work down through your body as you have done in Exercises 1 and 2. Read the following guidelines first and memorise them, or record them, or have someone read them to you.

As you sit comfortably in the chair do not cross your legs. Be aware of the sensations as you connect with the surface areas of your body.

Is your head resting on the back of the chair? What does that chair surface feel like against your head? Is it soft or hard? Warm or cool? Find your own words.

Notice the hair around your head and face. What does that feel like on your scalp?

Think about your back against the chair. How does your back feel as it rests against the chair? Is it hard or soft? Feel the textures against your body.

Now notice what it feels like to have the clothes on your back against your skin

Think about how your arms feel wherever they are resting. What sensation can you feel with your arms on the armrests or on your lap? What is the surface like against your arms?

Notice the material of your clothes against the skin on your arms. What does that feel like?

Focus on your bottom and how it feels on the seat of the chair. Is the chair seat soft or hard?

Now concentrate on your legs. Think about your thighs being supported by the chair. How does that feel? How do your calves feel as they press against the chair or where they have no direct support, what does the air around your calves feel like?

Think about your feet in your footwear. What can you feel there? Check on your toes and see what they feel like. Now think about your feet being supported by the floor. What can you feel there?

Relax for as long as you are able.

Now jot down a few notes about what you experienced.

Were there areas of your body where you could not discern the sensations? If so where?

If you repeat these exercises regularly you will become more and more in tune with your body sensations. And as you become more aware, you will begin to differentiate between sensations. You will develop the ability to know what biological hunger pangs feel like and what are psychological pangs. You can then explore what it is that you really need because if it is a psychological hunger you are feeling, food is not the answer.

This reconnection with the body self is a good aim for everyone. We have all lost some of the art of knowing through our bodily sensations as well as our minds. We can all miss sensations that tell us someone doesn't feel safe to be with, or that tell us that we are in the wrong place, that we don't want to do something we are being pushed to do and so forth. We feel some bodily sensations that we unconsciously ignore or discount instead of interpreting them. This is, of course, what happens when we interpret psychological hunger as biological hunger and eat.

When we look at those times when we eat food that we don't want to eat because someone or something, from past or present, is compelling us, we can check out what our bodies are telling us. We need to tune into our bodies and allow them to help us know what we need.

The fourth exercise is reconnecting with your body in a different way. If you are someone who doesn't use a mirror this will feel like a hard task. Some people feel anxious when asked to do this exercise. When we are in a room together, I can provide safety and support but that is not possible when reading it in a book. You have choices. You can get a trusted buddy, friend or relative, to be with you. You can do it on your own, stopping if you feel too much agitation to carry on. You can get professional help or you can decide not to do it at all. You can listen to it on my website www. myfoodspace.co.uk. It is entirely up to you. If you have a buddy she/he can read it out, otherwise, read it first and work through as much as you can.

You need to use a full-length mirror.

Exercise 4

Sit quietly for a while. Breathe deeply two or three times. When you are ready, move towards the mirror. Don't stand in front of it yet.

Firstly, from the side of the mirror, peep at yourself, as if playing peekaboo. Do this a few times and then smile and look at your smile in the mirror.

Now put one arm in front of the mirror and look at it. Move round to the other side and put the second arm in the mirror. Smile and then look at your smile in the mirror.

Now do the same with your leg and foot. Put one leg in front of the mirror. Look at it and smile, then look at your smile in the mirror.

Then stand on that leg and put the other leg in front of the mirror and when you are ready smile and look at your smile in the mirror.

Now put the left half of your body in front of the mirror and when you are ready, lean over to put your head in front of the mirror and smile. Then do the same with the other side of your body. Smile and look at your smile in the mirror.

Now, if you feel ready, stand with your whole body in front of the mirror. Look at your face and smile.

You are now going to look at your whole body in the mirror. Remember this body has been your friend and protector for some lengthy time. It has had a real purpose in your life. Maybe you won't need it like this much longer or maybe you will know that it is the right size for you. Treat it as a friend, albeit a friend you will be saying goodbye to if and when the time is right.

Stand in front of the mirror. Look at the areas of your body you like. Look at different parts of your body. Each part functions for you in some way. Maybe each part tells you something important. Let it tell you what that is.

Make friends with each part. Say: "you have been there for a reason, thank you".

Move nearer to the mirror so that you can look into your own eyes. Say "You are good", and "though you are bigger than I want you to be, you have been there because I needed you". Say "goodbye for now" and slowly move yourself out of the mirror.

Sit and breathe and relax for a while.

When you are ready, jot down some notes on what you have experienced and what you feel about your experience.

Now take a moment to reflect on what you have written. Write a few words about your reflections.

As you repeat these exercises and become more connected with your body sensations there will be three major consequences.

1. You will have much more idea of when you are biologically hungry and, even more specifically, when you have had enough to eat so that you can stop before you are over-full.
2. You will be able to detect discomforting sensations that tell you something is going on that you don't want and you will come to interpret those feelings more accurately. This in turn will help you to make new decisions about your eating and weight.
3. You will see your larger body as the protection it has given you and that you are working towards maybe not needing that kind of bodily protection anymore.

In summary

When you are being asked to do something you really don't want to do and is not right for you, your body may well be "the part of you" that lets you know this even when your mind is telling you that you must adapt and comply regardless. You can relate this to agitation in your Child ego-state. When you get those body sensations , you can use your Adult to work out what's happening. Then you can use that same Adult to find the right response for you.

You may remember that in the chapter about whether you are hungry for food or something else, I said your body sensation will help you to know which it is. So, these exercises practised regularly, will help you to attune to your body so that you will have much more idea about how you are using food other than for fuel to manage your day. Be really aware of your body self and you will be more aware of your psychological self. Your body self deserves attention. We can all discount all or parts of our body and that means we are discounting parts of ourselves.

Remember mind and body are as one. Be in tune with your body sensation and you will have an incredibly wise and helpful indicator of what you need, not just in respect of eating and weight but in other areas of your life too.

Chapter 12

The food distancing technique

I have already briefly introduced you to the idea of putting "distance" in time between your impulse and urge to eat and the action of eating. In this chapter, I am going to expand on this technique. Each time you come to use this tool, connect with what you think and feel when you:

a. **Think about using this technique**
b. **When you start to use this technique**
c. **When you have used this technique for the first time.**
d. **When you have used this technique a few times.**

The time lapses you create have two major functions: One is to get accustomed to waiting and deciding whether you need to eat at that moment or whether you (your Child) can wait; the other is to provide time for you to reflect on what you are feeling, what has just happened prior to reaching for something to eat, to explore the psychological hunger that is forcing you to use food.

You may want to keep an ongoing record of this on the pages at the back of the book headed "Food distancing Log". You will then see your progress as you use the technique more and more. Alternatively, you could use the App I have developed: "Myfoodspace" to help you put increasing time lapses between the impulse to eat and the action of eating which also logs your progress.

The reason I am asking you to do this technique is that, as you now know, there are psychological reasons for your unwanted weight, size and overeating and these may come to the fore when using this way of helping yourself to eat less. If you have been overweight for many years or are very overweight this will take time. Do this when you are ready or have a go and see what happens. There is no suggestion of "failure". If you get so far and then take a break, try to resume at the level you stopped at. Or maybe just a couple of stages earlier; that is your choice. Don't think about going backwards. Whatever happens, this is a journey forward. As we have already learnt, blips can be seen as part of that journey.

DOI: 10.4324/9781003240877-12

The route, again, may be along what can sometimes be a bumpy road. You need to get over those bumps when you are strong enough and know how to do so. You are using this book to find out about those bumps and ways of getting over them. You may need to just remain at the stage of time-lapse you have achieved for a while, whilst you discover what your psychological needs are.

If you achieve a satisfying length of time-lapse and then stop using the technique, be aware that you might be sabotaging your journey as you discovered in chapter 5. Always ask yourself why you would stop if it was working for you. If you don't' feel it has worked for you at all, ask yourself why this might be.

You can use this technique at any time, so let's think about occasions when you might eat that extra food and when using the technique might prove helpful.

1. Snacking between meals and between snacks.
2. When alone.
3. When challenged.
4. When annoyed with someone.
5. When unacknowledged.
6. When watching TV
7. When in the cinema.
8. When preparing food.
9. When in the car on the way somewhere.
10. When out for lunch or dinner.
11. When eating at home and taking seconds or thirds.
12. When eating up everything on your plate.
13. When finishing off the leftovers.
14. When someone wants to lure you into eating.
15. At a come-again buffet.

Tick the ones you recognise as times you reach for extra food and then add some of your own here.

At times, we also create an association between two things such as a coffee and a biscuit; a program on TV and crisps; Tea and cake; arriving home and snacking; Dinner then pudding. There is often a compulsion to have that biscuit with a coffee but you can use this technique to break such associations. So keep alert to the associations you have made; they are not always obvious but once you set yourself the mission to discover what they are they will become apparent. When we **automatically** enter into these associations, such as having that biscuit with coffee or tea, we are not using our Adult ego-state. When we consciously decide whether to have a biscuit or not, we are using Adult energy.

What are your associations? Write them here when you recognize them.

Now think about having a choice and stopping for a moment so that you can decide what to do in future.

You can also use this technique whilst shopping. You are most likely putting chocolates, crisps, snacks, or whatever your extra food is, into your basket without really thinking about it. This technique will help you to gradually stop and decide whether you want that foodstuff as the time-lapse grows. The important word here is "decide". We think of the word "decide" as an Adult word. Buying, or not buying, these extras is a significant part of your journey. You can aim to decide what to buy in your Adult rather than being driven by your Child. You still have the choice of buying them if you decide to. Use this technique, or the App, to help you. It is a discrete action. No one else will know you are stopping because you are on your journey. You can make your choices after just a second of consideration. If you find it tricky to get into your Adult on this one, remember you can use your posture to help you by standing straight with your head up and taking a "deepish" breath. That in itself will take a second so you are at the first stage of the technique already! Register your progress when shopping as part of your log at the back of the book.

(In the next chapter, you will find further ideas about shopping.)

As you have worked through the book this far, you will have understood more and more what the underlying issues are that prevent you from being the size and weight you want to be. This technique goes hand in hand with what you have discovered already.

The first stages of putting this time-distancing between the impulse to eat and the action of eating are only for a second and then a few more seconds. In the beginning, you would only have to wait one second before you eat what you were reaching for. You are not telling yourself you cannot eat whatever it is, your child can have the food, but you are just seeing if your Child can wait a moment. In that moment, you can see if she/he really wants or feels she/he needs it right now. It is important that your Child does not feel deprived, so you tell him or her she can have the food but that, together, (Parent, Adult and Child) you will just wait a moment. If the Child does feel agitated by this waiting, you can reassure him or her and then you can investigate that agitation as we have done in the chapters so far. Be curious about it. Usually, children are naturally curious and so might your Child be.

If this technique raises anxiety, agitation or fear at a level that feels overwhelming, then I advise you to seek professional help. However, because you will be using intervals of only seconds after which you can eat, your agitation might be short-lived.

Be sure to praise (Stroke) yourself after each step. You could provide yourself with a non-food reward system. Build up points or gold stars. Promise yourself a desirable award when you achieve a certain number of points or have paused for a minute or more for the first time. Make the reward fun or a relaxing treat and if possible, something other than food.

The technique

When you are aware that you are reaching for extra food, whether it is a snack, seconds or thirds at mealtime, when preparing food, or any other time I invite you to wait for just a second, then you can eat it. And the reason why you can eat it is so that you do not deny your Child what she/he needs. The important aspect is that your Child has waited one second to get what she/he wants or needs and does not feel deprived. You will gradually build up your time-lapse which then gives you time to recognise what is going on for you. It might be you start to recognise that psychological hunger we discussed in Chapter 9. You will have time to connect with the body sensations that can tell you what it is you need and that the need is not food.

There are a number of aims when using this technique:

1. To put increasing distance between the impulse to eat and the action of eating until such time as you are used to making decisions in this time-space as to whether you really want to take that food at that time or whether you can wait. Eventually, when you have reached a long time-lapse between impulse and action you may even not want it at all.
2. That you develop a time-lapse which is long enough for you to know what is causing that urge to eat. A time-lapse in which you can discover what it is you really need.
3. When shopping, you create a space to assess what you are buying.

So when you are aware you are heading for the biscuit tin, the fridge, the freezer, the leftovers, another snack, the cake, the chocolate (whatever your desire is), then you wait a second. Literally, in the beginning, you only need to wait one second. You can then continue to eat. This may sound easy to do, after all a second is such a brief length of time. But if the urge is strong, the Child energy can be very forceful and not listen to you saying "wait one second" even if you have "promised" the Child she/he can have the food after a brief pause. So, if you get to achieve that first step of waiting one second you should feel pleased and congratulate yourself. You now have a foundation on which to gradually build.

After achieving a one-second delay:
Notice what happens.
Was that hard?

Was that easy?

How do you feel about doing this?

How does your Adult see this action?

Whatever you feel is OK. You must be interested and intrigued by your response as I would be interested and intrigued if I could actually work with you. We would talk together about your experience and that is something you can do for yourself; you can talk to a buddy or yourself about that experience.

Remember you have a Child self who may feel agitated and a Nurturing Parent who can offer support, encouragement, understanding and love and you have an Adult who can observe everything and decide what is best to do next. Your Adult self can listen to your Child and make the right choices as you would with a real child in front of you.

Whatever you notice is important and useful information about what you need to do in order to change your behaviours and needs around eating and weight. Without that sort of information, it would be difficult to move forward.

You have now tried a 1-second wait and the world didn't fall apart! See if you can increase this time gap next time you get that urge.

Next time wait 2 seconds. Try these words to help you judge the 2 seconds: "One thousand and one, One thousand and two". As long as you pronounce each word deliberately and don't rush them, you will have waited 2 seconds. You can add on as you increase the time, of course: "A thousand and one, a thousand and two, a thousand and three," and so on. Or you can use a timer on your phone or clock, or you can use the "Myfoodpsace" App which will time for you and help you with reflections, advice and tasks.

Each time you do this, reflect on what you think and feel. Write down your reflections in your log pages at the back of the book. Each time you use the technique:

a.   Either stay at the time you have achieved so far, repeat it and really anchor that same time-lapse for a while. There is no hurry.
b.   Or increase the time a little more. You should increase in intervals of a second when you start so that your Child gets used to this process and is not alarmed.

Remember after you have achieved each time-lapse you can eat the food if you still want it but be sure that your Adult says it is OK to eat it. Your Child will then trust you.

When you get to a longer time gap you can start to really be in touch with what is happening for you. You may not need to do this for the entire time-lapse but you do need to be in touch with your sensations as you wait. Be interested and intrigued. You will gradually learn what is driving you to have this impulse to eat using all the information you have digested throughout the book. Write down what you discover each time. Don't ponder too long. You will build up your understanding over time. You can then check out this understanding in the previous chapters. It is very important to start to be aware of what happens immediately before you get that urge to eat. This might be psychological e.g. a psychological hunger(chapter 9) or a reaction to an injunction, (chapter 8) or it might be that something stressful or disappointing has just happened and you are reaching for food to quell feelings. Whatever it is, be interested and never judgemental.

As you aim to increase the time-lapse further and you have contacted your body sensation and begun to make some sense of it, you may want to find something to fill the gap. This will be helpful in extending the time distance between your impulse and action. There are many options. I am sure you can create your own. The App "Myfoodspace" has tasks and puzzles to help.

So here are some suggestions:

A. **Breathing Exercises**

You can use a breathing exercise for one or many seconds and even extend it to minutes.

If you have breathing problems or get dizzy if you take deep breaths, choose a different exercise. You must be responsible for yourself and make the appropriate choice. Since you are starting out with these few seconds towards a minute gap, (or longer) you can do any of these at work or at home. If you are somewhere where it is not appropriate to do some of the exercises then choose others or, if singing, for instance, just do it in your head.

When you are pausing for a few seconds up to 1 minute:
Read through the exercise first and then:

Sit and close your eyes, if that is OK for you, otherwise focus on a spot on the wall. Take a really good deep breath and then slowly let it go. Do this again and on the third time take in a more moderate breath and imagine that breath entering your body, going down into your lungs so that your rib cage expands and tummy pushes out. Notice that happening in your body. Then very slowly puff out through your lips and make the outbreath as long as you can and as long as is comfortable for you. Then just concentrate on your normal breathing.

You can repeat this as you need to and you can use your Adult to make a decision about eating whatever it is you wanted to reach for. This exercise will also help you to relax, which in turn lowers any agitation present.

When you are pausing for a minute or longer:
Read through the exercise first and then:

Sit as above, eyes closed or focussed on the wall. Slowly take one good deep breath and let it out gradually. Now imagine you are taking in a beautiful relaxing light as you take a slow deep breath in. Imagine this beautiful light travelling through and around your head, into your neck and down into your chest and back. As you breathe normally, let this light travel down into your tummy and thighs. Imagine that bright warm light circling around and soothing your body.

Now imagine that light leaving through your feet as you inhale another deep breath of bright and beautiful light. Repeat for as long as you want.

This exercise is very relaxing and relaxation enables you to think more clearly. It stops the buzzing messages in the head.

B. **Mantras and reciting**

Do these out loud if you possibly can otherwise do them in your head. Stay focussed.

1. Repeat your four mantras:	**I am worth it!** **I am OK** **I can think** **I have choices and can decide for myself**
2. Or use this little rhyme:	I know I have worth I'm OK I'm sure I've been that from birth It's there in my core I know I can think And know I can choose I decide for myself. And that's really good news!

3. Make up your own rhyme to use at these times.
4. Maybe you could sing a song or recite a nursery rhyme out loud or to yourself.
5. If you are a puzzler, you could start a puzzle.

The app also provides things for you to do.

Add your own ideas as to what would be helpful to you:

1.
2.
3.

When you increase your gap time to 4 or 5 minutes you can do something else. The possibilities are endless.

Here are some suggestions but you can definitely find your own.

1.   Write something. This takes you into your Adult. It could be your thoughts. It could be a job list, a shopping list of your choice of favourite healthy foods, a list of people you need or want to contact or who you haven't seen for ages. Make a phone call. Go outside for a look around. Maybe notice nature, birds, shrubs, trees, the wind, rain, sun etc. If at work, you could do the same or similar distracting tasks. Be sure to be aware of your time-lapses.
2.   Do a quick job in the house like washing up, or putting the washing out, vacuum a room, or if at work, find something appropriate to do, maybe chat to a colleague for this short time or nip to the loo.
3.   Read something: your book, a paper, or magazine or something that is available, appropriate or needed whether at work or at home.
   Add a few of your ideas here. Give yourself a variety to choose from.

1.

2.

3.

4.

When you move beyond 5 minutes waiting time you will probably find that you are not clock-watching in the same way. However, I do encourage you to keep track of the time so that you can see your progress. Imagine yourself being able to do something else other than eating that food for 5 and then 10 minutes or more? Amazing!

At any stage, you can still time yourself knowing that you can have that food if you want it. However, you might want to ask yourself:

Do I still want this food?

Do I want it now?

Can I wait until later?

Can I wait until my next mealtime?

Why would I feel I can't wait?

How do I feel about this?

You can use these questions each time you use the technique.

Keep a record of your timings in the log at the back of the book together with your thoughts, sensations and reflections.

Remember: There is no such thing as failure, you may just encounter a blip. As I have said before, the blip becomes a valid part of the journey. Each time you get to a longer waiting time you have to remind yourself that you got there and that stage of achievement cannot be taken away from you. You may need to build up again, but so what? This is not a race; it is a gentle journey towards change. Every different step, no matter how small, is an achievement and deserves recognition. Praise yourself for what you do and don't harp on what you don't do. We all have days when we revert to some other behaviour! One or two blips don't mean you have failed or that there is no point continuing. If you got to 3 minutes, for instance, and then had a blip, that 3 minutes becomes your personal best, your PB. That can't be taken away. So next time you start from 3 minutes or you may want to start a couple of stages earlier and then get to and try to exceed your PB. That new time-lapse will then become your PB which cannot be taken away. This way you will have more confidence to continue.

Once you have reached a 15-minute pause between that impulse to eat and the action of eating you are very much at the point of a new way of being. Continue to grow the time lapses until you are thinking that you could wait until later to eat, wait for your next meal, you might even wait until tomorrow. The food is not going to go away. You might even forget that you were going to eat!

Be kind to yourself. Think positively about what you achieve each time. Be observant about the times you don't manage the longer gaps and write down your thoughts and feelings in the Technique log at the back of the book. Use other chapters to explore your feelings and sensations that may arise in the time-lapse. Praise yourself for what you achieve and write these praises down. Give yourself positive strokes.

The first goal, then, is clearly to put that distance in time between the urge to eat and the action of eating and to increase the time-lapse.

The second goal is to break the habit such that you no longer need to time yourself. You may feel the urge and you will use your Adult to decide what you want to do. **Once you have reached 15–30 minutes** you will almost certainly no longer respond from a deprived or agitated Child self, particularly if you have reflected on what your psychological needs are in that time-lapse space. You will have used your Adult to stop impulsive or compulsive eating and will have an informed choice. You will be able to take care of yourself in a new and positive way.

You will be able to consider your reflections and the thoughts and feelings you have noted down and use the appropriate chapters in this book to aid your understanding. Check out when your Parent, Child and Adult are in operation throughout this journey.

You will know you are in Adult when you use adult thinking and assessment, when you use the language of an adult person, when your body is in a grown-up position, not slumped over as if defeated or withdrawing like a frightened toddler but with your head up and your back straight. Your tones will be clear and straightforward with an air of potency. You will be able to reason with your Child self.

The time-lapse gives you the space to consider what it is you need when you recognise that it isn't food. Do not chastise yourself if you eat before the desired time lapse is up; just be sure to check what is happening in your body or what has just actually occurred before your agitation leads you to reach for food.

Above all be interested, intrigued and enjoy this part of your journey. It is fun and rewarding.

Chapter 13

The power you give to food

In this chapter, I hope to help you recognise the power you give to food and to change that power so that you are the controller. You can take back your power by understanding what food is doing for you and what you are doing with food. This chapter focuses on a further helpful way of thinking about food.

Food clearly does not have power; we give it power until it feels like it beckons, entices, rules, controls and takes away our strength to refuse it.

As we have seen in other chapters, the Child in us is the part that feels the magnetism of food or has chosen to eat as a way of attempting to escape from adversity or to feed psychological hunger. It is the Child that is the impulsive and compulsive eater.

We have discussed before in this book the three possible functions of food in this context. One is purely biological and two are psychological. Of these psychological needs, one relates to food and eating per se and the other relates to the maintenance of the larger, unwanted, body size. Of the two types of psychological needs for food, then, one is that food is used as a bid to resolve both unconscious and conscious fears and doubts about one's self, others or one's world; And the other is that food is eaten to maintain a larger size which feels like a protective layer, a shield, against fears and doubts and what the world has thrown, and still seems to throw, at us.

They both require eating "extra" food but in one instance it is the food itself that is the tool and in the other, it is the large body size that matters.

When it feels we are in need of food for psychological reasons, that food, whatever it is, becomes very powerful. It is like we cannot do anything other than eat at these uncomfortable or distressing times. It often feels that we have no say in whether at these times we eat or not. We do not listen to the positive Nurturing Parent self or the Adult self saying that there might be better ways of dealing with the problems than the Child's desperation to eat. Food can feel like an answer and a saviour at these times, and in this lies its power. Even if we do hear those voices saying "this is not the answer" we can speedily dismiss and reject them.

DOI: 10.4324/9781003240877-13

I recently had a stressful encounter and "found myself" reaching for food. I put "found myself" in inverted commas because it does feel like I had no say in the matter, but actually, as we have considered before, we always have choices. The truth is I didn't just "find myself" doing this, I actually made a conscious and an unconscious decision to do it from a very agitated Child place. It seemed that I was desperate and it felt as though I was rushing to stuff something into my mouth before the helpful messages found the needed words in my head. Not only that, but when that part of me was subsequently saying "This isn't the way to resolve this" and "you will regret this later", I "found myself" telling those voices in no uncertain terms to go away and leave me alone. Such is the power of food. If you find yourself saying "I found myself doing...." then accept that there is no such thing as "finding oneself" doing something, there is always a choice and a decision involved, whether conscious or unconscious. As long as we accept this, we can learn to do something different. I was able to put that moment of time between my impulse and action and reduce the power that food seemed to have.

It is at these times that I use the technique described in the previous chapter. The initial time gap, albeit just a second long, already started to calm my Child.

The need at these times is about immediacy and we don't normally give ourselves time to think, we just need to act upon the urge to eat. When you think about this now, do you think you have had these similar circumstances where the need to eat just takes over and nothing will stop you from eating?

In therapy clients find it really fascinating to literally look at the type of foods they might reach for that are not for their biological hunger. You could do the same. What do the foods you reach for remind you of? Are there certain colours, textures or flavours that particularly appeal to you at these times? One of my client's, George, also found this thought-provoking. He put some of his favourite snacks in front of him and introduced himself to each of them. This, he felt almost immediately, seemed to "put some equality" in the relationship between him and those foods whereas previously he felt the food had the overbearing power. He then talked to each of them, asking each one what it thought it did for him.

Here is what George reported: some were silent and he concluded that these were the ones that he probably used less. He really felt that others were replying. Chocolate had a very alluring and persuasive voice and seemed to think it was George's saviour. Crisps were indignant that he should be asking and just said things like "you can't do without me!" The cake was a little more complex. This seemed to be because it said there were lots of people to eat it and George only needed a small slice but this was followed by an assurance that George would definitely have more. It wanted George to feel full. When George "conversed" with his chips, he seemed to become immersed and for a while found it difficult to separate himself from them. He realised that the other foods could effectively wait to be eaten, whereas the chips needed to be eaten quickly and whilst hot. George had difficulty resisting and messages like "you can't waste me" came into his mind.

George engaged what he felt to be his Adult self and over a period of time, he was able to argue with these foods that they were not essential to him and that he would choose when he would have them. He told them that he realised that they did not resolve anything for him and in fact, made things worse. In doing this he felt his own potency, taking back the power he had given to those foods.

Even though this might seem quite bizarre it might be something you would be willing to try. If you enter the spirit of the exercise, the "replies" from the foods will come to you. You can either line up some foodstuffs, as George did, or you could do this with each snack item individually at any time. You could just make a list of your snack foods and address each of them to see what message you receive from them. It is an interesting exercise if you are willing to do it.

Write down here what foodstuffs you will "have a discussion with."

When you have had your discussion, write down what you heard the food say.

What is your Adult assessment, response and decision?

You will find it helpful to do this exercise regularly so that you get to know what each food's role is. Each time you do it, keep a record of what happens. If you feel agitated, as some do when thinking about doing this exercise, you may not wish to continue but you can reflect on why you might feel this agitation. Clients who have felt this have been concerned that this would lead to those foods being "taken away". This is not the case. You will always have a choice. When you are ready you will eat them less often.

The foods that people choose in an attempt to resolve psychological issues are indeterminate. Sometimes it needs to be a certain texture, soft, hard, substantial, chewy, crispy, sometimes a certain taste but sometimes it just needs to be a large quantity. We can easily kid ourselves that a plate of food is not "unhealthy" but the power is in the huge amount on the plate. In this case, it is perhaps the amount of food that has the power rather than the food itself.

When a stressful, taxing or challenging thing happens you may feel compelled to eat whatever food you can get in order to try to feed that hunger. It might not be the snack type foods but just any food. I have known people who will take food out of the waste bin when the urge is so strong. Psychological hungers are very persuasive. For instance, when you feel sad, lonely, unheard or unseen, and the pain of that is with you, you might reach for food to placate those feelings. Food feels like your friend and then afterwards it often feels like the enemy. The compulsion to eat seems to have its own power. At these times you are not thinking rationally, that is to say, you are not able to allow your Adult rational thinking because the need to respond to those painful feelings is so great that the Adult self is barred from the process.

The Child wants the food and wants it now. Sometimes it really does feel like a matter of survival, of life and death, the painful feelings can be so strong. At such times if you tell your Child she/he can't have the food, she/he will up the ante until she/he gets it!

We often reach for food in an emotional and psychological "emergency". There is no real emergency. There is usually food in the cupboards and fridge and there are usually shops less than half an hour away. So, when your Child feels in a panic for food, she/he needs soothing and reassuring. She/he needs to be reassured that there isn't a food shortage so she/he doesn't have to panic.

Although the impulse to eat comes from within our psychologically needs, it is food that we give power to as if it can resolve our issues. We don't normally think of food in this way until it is brought into awareness.

Let's reflect now:

First of all, just be aware of those times when you reach for food without thinking about whether you need it or not. Think about the times you feel a panic that drives you to eat; about times when you recognise that it seems you have no power to say no; you MUST have something to eat! At these times the food has the ultimate power; you give it the power to soothe you; you give it the power to "resolve" something in you; you give it the power to always have the power because you will never feel it has done the job for more than a very brief space of time. You may even eat more just to be sure you won't feel deprived. The boost you feel is so often short-lived and, repeatedly, there are feelings of regret or even self-loathing after eating. As long as psychological hungers remain unresolved there will be the next time and the next time where you hand over your power to chocolate, crisps, cake, biscuits, takeaways or whatever your chosen food is at these times.

Questions for you:

When you have eaten what do you feel?

Do you feel better?

For how long do you feel better?

Do you feel angry with yourself?

Do you feel disappointed in yourself?

Do you feel full, or sick, or distended or uncomfortable?

Most of all, has your painful feeling such as sadness, or emptiness gone away for more than those minutes you were eating? I suspect the answer is "no"

So let's look at some ways in which you might gradually take back some of that power.

Write down all your thoughts and feelings when you recognise that you have just given over your power to food.

Now, as you look at your list, underline all the thoughts and feelings that are helpful to you. Then write them here. If none are helpful from that list, write at least three thoughts and feelings that will help you in future.

Repeat this exercise as often as you can. Each time you do, you will find there are new responses arising. Keep comparing your notes and always be curious about what this means for you and how you can help yourself with the new knowledge you are gathering.

Below is a summary of ways in which you can discover and take back the power you are giving to food.

1.   Talk with the food on your plate or in the serving dishes. (Again, you can do this in your head if you don't want to say it out loud.) Tell the food you appreciate that it is there for you but that you do not need it all at one time. Tell it you can save it for later or tomorrow. Tell it you know that it is trying to lure you into eating it but that you are not giving in to it. Tell it you can decide whether you eat it or not and that you are stronger than it.

2.   Like George, ask the food what it does for you. You can "listen" to the response that occurs in your head as if the food is talking. This is an immensely powerful exercise, even though it seems rather bizarre.

3.   Ask the food why it feels it is important that you eat it. Listen to the words that come into your head. Be intrigued. Talk with the food as if you have the upper hand. Thank it for being there for you and that you will make informed decisions about it from now on.

4.   Talk to the biscuits, the cakes, the crisps and chocolate and anything else that you often don't feel able to resist. Ask them questions about what it is there for and then negotiate with it. You could negotiate when you might eat that food so that you set out your own timetable for eating it. This negotiating gives you the upper hand in the discussion.

5.   When you think you want another helping, why not tell the food you will wait and see if you really want it and that you will make that decision and let it know what you have decided.

6.   Add your own ideas below or in the pages at back of the book.

When shopping

1.   When you are drawn to the counters where there are the temptations you recognise as being your nemesis, talk to them. Say "thanks for being there and I know you will be there another day when I come in, so I will leave you there for today."

2.   Say "I am going to take some of you home but not as many as normal. I don't need you all the time. You are not going to control me; I shall take charge now".

3. Think about when you will be shopping next. Is it really necessary to take home lots of food as if there will be none left another day? Reassure yourself that the food will be there tomorrow and the next day and so on.
4. Pick a couple of unhelpful foods that you normally buy and say "I am going to see what happens if I don't buy you today."
5. If you are popping into a filling station and are tempted to buy chocolate or snacks, ask yourself if you really want something or has this mode of buying snacks when filling the car just become a habit. Make an Adult decision about whether you will buy stuff today.
6. Think of your own words to say to those extras when out shopping and tempted to buy lots of snack foods. Jot down some ideas here.

When eating out

Does eating out feel like a special occasion and therefore warrants eating a lot of food? If you eat out often, ask yourself why you would want extra food and maybe alcohol just because you are out. Does that make sense to you? Can you still enjoy yourself without overindulging? Ask yourself these questions and then keep "the discussion" going in your head until you feel satisfied with your Adult-reasoned answer. If you start to feel angry, agitated or panic, then you are not in your Adult. Your Child, and thereby the food, are in control.

You can *decide* to buy snacks and eat the extra foods and drink the extra alcohol if that is what your Adult has concluded. No one wants to be stuffy about this. The point is to think about it and then make **an informed decision** rather than relinquishing the power you have to make a coherent choice. In other words, you are not automatically reaching for food or drink without Adult thought.

I really like these ways of thinking about how we give food the power and how we might take back that power. Part of the appeal is that it has a playful and charming note to it which fascinates the Child.

Talking to the foods as described above is a useful activity when putting time distance between the impulse to eat and the action of eating as described in Chapter 12.

Chapter 14

The place of body and movement in your journey

In Chapter 11, you read about ways of reconnecting with your body self through focusing on sensations within the different parts of the body. In this chapter, we look at moving the body to increase this awareness and to release blocked energy.

The aim of body movement is to release energy that has been blocked in the musculature by challenging and traumatic experiences in childhood, and indeed, throughout life. The body has its own memory and movement has been proven to allow for freedom in the body, and thereby, associated freedom in the mind. When the connection with our body self is lost, that movement and flow of energy are extremely limited. I have found that moving, preferably with music, and exploring what the body can do, has been extremely beneficial to my clients who have come with their struggle with weight as their presenting issue. This is for a number of reasons:

1. People struggling with their weight are inclined to hold tension in their bodies and often do not move all their body parts. By simple movement that tension can be released.
2. Some overweight people believe they can't move their bodies sufficiently to gain any benefit from it. This is not true. Even the smallest movement can shift blocked energy.
3. Moving the body as freely as possible enables people to claim their space in the world in ways other than having to be a large size.
4. In the release that comes from movement, clients have discovered the emotion that has also been blocked and have, therefore, been able to let it go.
5. Movement allows the body to "speak". We can make meaning from the areas of the body that are stiff, painful, or without recognised sensation.
6. Moving releases energy that is waiting to be released.

The exercises that you learnt in Chapter 11 will also help with this release of energy.

There are two ways of thinking about movement. One is directed movement, where we "impose" movement on the body and the other is a

DOI: 10.4324/9781003240877-14

movement driven by the unconscious. In the latter, we wait and see what the body wants to do. In the former, we tell the body what to do.

It may seem strange to say, but some overweight people need to find their bodies first. This means that they need to accept their body rather than discounting it by refusing to see it, touch it, watch it, move it, or sense it as part of the self.

Whatever the reason for overeating or maintaining an unwanted large body size, movement is another key element in your journey. Simple movement in the directions your body naturally goes should be OK for you but, if in doubt, take the book to your GP and check that there will be no problem in moving as described below. Take care of yourself by being sure.

It is helpful to move to your favourite music. Music is in our collective consciousness and was perhaps originally inspired by the heartbeat and sounds in nature. Music is within us all and, if we let it, it can move us both physically and emotionally.

I suggest initially that you use soft, slow, soothing music. This will help you to relax into the movements. These movements are meant for everyone. Read through the exercises and choose the ones that seem right for you. The first ones encourage free movement, starting with ideas for tracing the space around you. You can take it where you want and explore that space. You can start with five minutes of movement and build up as much as you want and as much as is comfortable for you. There is no competition; just time to concentrate on yourself (you will also find these exercises recorded for you on the website "myfoodspace").

(Only do these exercises if you feel you can move in these ways. You are responsible for your choice to do them or not.)

Exercise 1

1. **Choose your soft music if you want to use it. Listen to your music for a moment. The music will suggest gentle movement.**
2. **Stand and very slowly open your arms wide. Then still with your arms wide, take a few steps in a circle feeling the space around you. Look at your arms to left and right. See them stretching into your space.**
3. **Now begin to push both arms outwards one side, leaning a little into this stretch. Do the same on the other side. Repeat three or four times.**
4. **Now begin to see what your body wants to do next. Just follow your unconscious directions. You may want to lean into your space in front, or reach up, or bend down. Whatever is right for you. Keep moving in the way your body tells you it wants to go.**

Feel you are claiming your space and place in the world.

5. Take large slow and controlled steps around your room, pushing your arms out into your own space. Let your body release and move in whatever direction it wants to go. Keep your body moving for as long as you and it wants to.

Sit for a few moments and let thoughts pass through your head, watch them as if on a screen, just passing through.

Repeat this exercise often, maybe changing the music as you see fit. There is no need to analyse what you do. Your body will know.

Exercise 2   Choose your gentle music again. This time kneel on the floor or sit on an easy chair that allows you to move.

1. Cross your right arm over your body as smoothly as you can and then with loose hands, inscribe an arc in front of you, stretching your arm forward and to the right. Watch your hand as it slowly travels. Then do the same with the other arm and hand. Repeat two or three times.
2. If you are able, lift your hands up to the ceiling. Watch your hands. Expand your chest. Hold there. Take two deep breaths and bring your arms slowly down watching your hands. Repeat these three or four times. (Do a half-reach without raising above your head if you have high blood pressure or sore shoulders or other restricting conditions.)
3. With your arms stretched out in front of you, bend forward as far as is right for you. Do this smoothly and slowly. Open your arms if you can and then draw them into your chest. Curl like a hedgehog. Gently release. Repeat.
4. Kneeling or sitting up, gently lead your outstretched right arm slightly behind you. Just as far as you can go. Watch your hand as far as you can. Then slowly bring it back and do the same on the other side. Repeat. Do not push too far. Small movement is just as good.

Now sit in a chair and take two deep and calming breaths, puffing the air out through your lips. Relax and reflect.

> **Exercise 3**   If you wish to have more lively music now, that is fine. Otherwise, stay with your gentle beat.
>
> In this exercise, you are going to stand if you are able (or sit if not) and let your body move wherever it wants to go. You must believe you can do this, and you can.
>
> Your body will move and you just need to follow it.
>
> Be aware of what your arms and hands want to do, then let them and your feet lead you.
>
> Make shapes with your arms and legs, your hands and your torso. Your body makes beautiful shapes. Explore the shapes your body can make and the way it can move through your room. Enjoy your body movements.
>
> Aim to do this for 4 or 5 minutes in the beginning and then sit and breathe deep breaths, puffing out through your lips as before. Relax. Reflect.

The exercises above are soothing and exploratory. There is no need for interpretation. You do not have to make meaning of them. Your body self and psychological self will know what these mean to you. They will work from within.

You move your body in numerous ways automatically throughout the day. If you exaggerate some of these natural movements, you will free your body that bit more. Here are some ideas:

Dust or polish a little more vigorously; "dance" around with the vacuum cleaner; scrub a little harder; clean tops with gusto; walk a little faster; if sitting at a table at work or home, flex your feet up and down, circle your ankles; do a few marches under the table; reach twice for the same cup; I am sure you are getting the idea. Just add a little, or exaggerate your, movement. You can do all this to music too. Whatever your daily routine is think about extending your body that bit further. If you have to take the lift, you could march on the spot or even use the stairs. If you are at a desk all day, set your alarm and stand up every hour and move for a minute or two. Think about how your body is meant to move and just push it a little more than normal. There is no need to go to extremes.

I will now suggest a few extra movements you can also include in your normal day. You don't have to go to classes or the gym. These are good movements gradually using the whole body. You might want to do them to music. We do so much lifting and stretching around the house and at work without even thinking about it. When we are thinking about and concentrating on our bodies and movement, we can see we are exercising and moving energy around the body. It is as simple as that. We are in the moment with ourselves.

Figure 14.1   Toe taps and leg lifts at a work top or holding on to a chair back.

Let's start at the sink where you might be washing things or worktop or bench where you might be working. Or you can hold on to a chair back.

1. **Tap your heel to the floor and then your toe. Heel-toe 5 or 6 times on one side and then the other.**
2. **Lift your right leg backwards 3 or 4 times, either bent or straight, whichever is right for you.**
3. **Lift your right leg to the side 3 or 4 times. Then do the same with the left leg. Get used to doing this each time you are in a position to do so** (Figure 14.1).

Over time you can increase the number of lifts and the number of repeats of each set. But start simply and build up.

4. **Now just turn your head and upper body slightly sideways as if looking at someone who has just walked into the room. Keep your hips facing forward if you can. This is a waist twist. Do it slowly twice on each side and then repeat as you see fit.**
5. **Lift your shoulders to your ears and relax; do this four times and build up. Roll your shoulders round. It feels good! Move them forwards and back and then relax.** A lot of tension sits in this head and shoulder area, so you are doing two useful things here: movement and tension release.
6. **Now think about when you walk around the house or workplace, go upstairs, or even when you go to the loo. Add a few extra movements.**

You can lift and bend your arms in front and into your chest, then open forwards and return to bent. Do this with one arm and then the other or both together. Repeat (Figure 14.2).

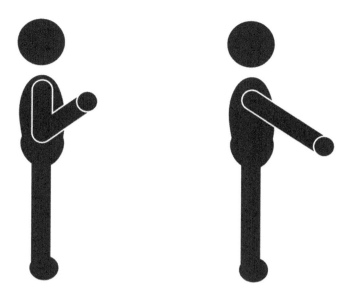

Figure 14.2 Arm straighten and bend.

7. **Watching the television. Practise a bent leg lift in the chair, first one side and then the other** (Figure 14.3).

Figure 14.3 Knee lifts.

You can lift heel and toe, do some foot circling, include arm lifts, head circling and shoulder lifts. (just warn whoever you are with that you are going to do a few unusual tele-watching moves; or better still, get them to do them too). Only do these if you feel it is right for you.

8.   Now is a good time to do some tummy exercises because no one will know. Just pull your tummy muscles in and hold. You will soon get used to the feel of it. Repeat about 4 times and then do the same later on. Again, build up. Tummy pulls are quite strong, so pace yourself. You can do these exercises wherever you are, in a queue, on the bus, in the car, at work, etc. Tummy tightening can be amazingly effective if done often enough, and no-one knows you are doing it!

I am sure you can see you are moving your body and exercising all day whether you want to or not and now you are adding conscious movements to ensure you are moving each part with focus. Once you get into doing this and recognise what you are doing, I hope you will find it interesting and enjoyable. You can add your own moves, of course. Once you start concentrating you will find all sorts of things you could do.

Movement and exercise lift your mood, enable connection with your body self, release blocked tension and use energy. Movement helps reshape your body. It keeps you supple and gets your joints moving. These simple movements are the way to start. There is no competition and no hurry. Be in tune with the release you feel as you focus on body movement. And above all, enjoy discovering your body again.

Chapter 15

Recapping, encouragement and concluding thoughts

Congratulations! You have now done an amazing amount of self-exploration, made new decisions about yourself, your past and those around you and begun to see how all this has driven you to overeat or carry a larger size body than you want. Even if you have done all the exercises, you will benefit again and again from rereading the chapters and repeating the exercises. This is because something new can occur to you each time you self-explore. It is as though each insight can open a door to further realisations that might be useful in your continued journey. The more you understand what is going on for you, consciously and unconsciously, the more you can take charge of your life, which includes your eating and weight.

If you have struggled with your weight and eating for many years, you will need to keep aware of all the elements that you have discovered so far. Awareness is key to you gaining the Adult control you need in order to continue your journey until it becomes second nature to refuse extra food, have less on your plate, choose foods that are healthy and right for you and stop using food in an attempt to resolve psychological issues. Eventually, that awareness will also become the norm for you. The food distancing technique is, of course, an important practical tool. If you ever feel you are reverting to old behaviours around eating, this is a good method to use to get you on track. First, it encourages you to wait a while before eating; secondly, it provides a space for your Adult to assess the situation; thirdly it allows you to reflect on why you feel you need to eat at that moment; and, fourthly, it gives you time to calm the Inner Child who is demanding the food. Any one of these reasons to use the technique can result in you postponing eating.

I do urge you to recap your answers to the questions in all the chapters. Keep an ongoing note of your thoughts, feelings, reflections and behaviours. Changing eating habits and losing weight takes time. As I said in chapter 4, a slow loss is paramount if you want the weight to stay off. It allows time to get accustomed to the different body sizes both physically and mentally. I have suggested 1–2 pounds or 0.5–1 kilo per week is enough to aim for whatever one's size and desired weight.

DOI: 10.4324/9781003240877-15

In the first part of the book, we looked at various mantras that make up the building blocks on which to start your journey. "I am worth it" was one such mantra. It may have been difficult to say it with conviction at that time but I suspect that by now you will have gained more confidence in this belief about yourself, especially if you have followed through all the chapters and completed the questions. You have only been able to dedicate this time to your journey if you have believed that you are worth it. Perhaps you can say it with more conviction now. I invite you to do so before you read on: **"I am worth it."**

I wonder if you have grappled with your sabotage? If so, what did you do about it? Was it interesting to see how you might have prevented yourself from continuing your journey? Did you discover the reason for those bumps in the road? Did your means of sabotage tally with what you wrote in chapter 5? Assuming you are not still in sabotage mode, congratulate yourself on getting over the bumps. That is a remarkable achievement and will stand you in good stead for the future. If you *are* now in sabotage mode, think about what it is you need in order to resume your journey and continue forward. It might be that a particular chapter helps you, so quietly spend a moment to see what comes to mind.

In the second part of the book, you encountered a much deeper exploration of your unconscious energies and motivations. If you decided to skip some of the questions because of feeling agitated you might now feel able to return to them. If they still feel painful seek help with a trained therapist or counsellor. (Always check qualifications before embarking on therapy.) Perhaps central to the second part of the book is the knowledge that what you are regularly experiencing is not biological hunger but psychological hunger. Biological hunger needs comparatively less food than most of us actually eat. Psychological hungers force us to eat far more than we need biologically to deal with the tasks (energy output) of the day. When we get to recognize the difference, we can make more appropriate choices to meet those hungers than reaching for food.

To differentiate between the two types of hungers, we need to be in contact with our bodies; hence we looked at how to connect, or reconnect, with the body self through various meditative exercises and body movement.

There is much for you to be proud of now that you have completed the first reading of this self-help book. Please continue to work with what you have learnt and the concepts I have introduced. Don't let all your effort be wasted. Recap with chapters in the book as this is a way of maintaining your changes. If you feel you are slipping back to old habits and losing the self-caring you have learnt then there is still a little more work to do. Find which chapter you related to most and go through the exercises again. Each time we do these exercises, more unconscious elements rise to consciousness. It is as though we learn in layers; once we have grasped one layer another one becomes available to us.

If you would like to contact a TA therapist or counsellor you will find them listed online. You just need to type in Transactional Analysis and your country and you will find a list of names with information about whether they work with eating and weight issues. Always choose a registered therapist; if they are registered with their organization, and/or with UKCP or BACP for instance, they will have the relevant training.

There are Transactional Analysts in countries all over the world. It is a movement that was started in the USA by Eric Berne and soon followed in the UK and then gradually went global. Many Psychotherapists will work online where they are not local to you.

If you would like to read more about TA, there are numerous books to be found in many languages. The core book in English for new students to TA is "TA Today" by Stewart and Van Joinnes (Life Space Publishing), if you wish to read additional theory. My book "The overweight Patient" Jessica Kingsley Publishers offers additional thinking about overeating and overweight issues. And my website "Myfoodspace.net" and my App "Myfoodspace" add further information and help.

Books on TA, eating and being overweight are rare. I personally am not familiar with any other current ones. There are, however, other resources that you might want to investigate, but only when you are ready. You might want to ask for the help of a dietician or nutritionist through your GP. Dieticians are a regulated body of certificated practitioners; nutritionists do not have this demand but there are well-trained nutritionists around. Always check qualifications and experience.

I do not advocate slimming groups because they are directive and what you have done in these chapters is develop your own capacity for self-direction and potency. However, if you feel you want to join a group, make sure it is the one for you and try a few sessions before committing yourself. Always attend in your Adult self so that you take control of what you eat and when, and you do so for yourself. If you find you are complying to please the leader or to not feel a failure in the group, your weight loss, as I am sure you will now recognise, will not be maintained. Make a clear and decisive choice and decision if you want to join a group, never go because you "should" or "ought" to.

I have deliberately not written about healthy eating as there is a great deal of information available about this in books and online. However, I sometimes think that the advice is a bit daunting because you are given so much information in one go. Find out bit by bit what foods are best for you and change your food intake slowly. Replace old for new. For instance, Yoghurt instead of cream, jacket potato instead of chips, chicken instead of burgers and so on. Gradually reduce fast-food purchases; if you change one thing every week you will soon achieve healthy eating habits that are right for you. Only ever choose alternatives that you like. If you find it difficult to find healthier substitutes just eat less of the things you are eating until you find foods that suit you better given the goals you have in mind.

For additional support, you may wish to read other material and investigate what is available to you online. There is an interesting website for a holistic approach to change which is Slimnastic.com. You will find information and books with appealing recipes if you are ready for those! Dr Rangan Chatterjee has also written helpful books with a whole-person plan to weight control and lifestyle. His latest (2021) is "Feel Great – Lose Weight" which can be found on Amazon.

Whatever you decide to do next, keep this book handy so you can always recap on things that might need another visit. Once you start branching out, more unconscious material may become conscious. Treat it as your friend and guide.

Thank you for using my book whether it is about your weight-loss journey or your discovery that you are OK as you are. I wish you every success in reaching your goals in life.

Appendix: Pages for your notes

a. Your thoughts, feelings and reflections on each chapter

Write the chapter heading and then write your thoughts, feelings and
reflections.

Your thoughts, feelings and reflections on each chapter

Write the chapter heading and then write your thoughts, feelings and reflections.

Your thoughts, feelings and reflections on each chapter

Write the chapter heading and then write your thoughts, feelings and reflections.

Your thoughts, feelings and reflections on each chapter

Write the chapter heading and then write your thoughts, feelings and reflections.

Your thoughts, feelings and reflections on each chapter

Write the chapter heading and then write your thoughts, feelings and reflections.

b. Your stroke collection

Keep a record of all the strokes you receive and give yourself and others. These can be anything from a nod, a smile, a "hello", a compliment etc.

c. Your food distancing technique log

Each time you increase the time lapse between the impulse to eat and the action of eating, starting from a one-second interval, write the date and the time-lapse you have achieved.

(If there are occasions when you don't reach your Personal Best that day, you may wish to write that down too, with the reason you didn't quite get there. This may help you in your journey forwards. Remember, there is no such thing as going backwards or failing!)

If this page becomes full, continue in your own notebook. Don't stop logging in until you feel confident you are in charge!

Date Time lapse	Date Time lapse	Date Time lapse

d. Body movement progress

Make a list of movements you have achieved, how many repetitions you have done, or the length of time you were moving.

Additional notes

For Product Safety Concerns and Information please contact our EU representative GPSR@taylorandfrancis.com Taylor & Francis Verlag GmbH, Kaufingerstraße 24, 80331 München, Germany

Printed and bound by CPI Group (UK) Ltd, Croydon, CR0 4YY
08/06/2025
01896986-0016